"Tyler Blanski beckons us to a 'holy renaissance' in *When Donkeys Talk*. He weaves together a many-threaded tapestry that calls us back to the 'deep magic' of a earthy, deeply abiding, and living faith where donkeys talk, the universe is filled with God, stars proclaim the birth of a King, and Jesus gives himself to us in creation through water, bread, and wine. He calls us to step out of the materialism of 'Atomland' and experience a sacramental universe filled by God and one wherein God dwells in us and we dwell in him."

— The Rev. T. L. Holtzen, PhD, Professor of Historical and Systematic Theology, Nashotah House

"Tyler Blanski has written an imaginative and persuasive apology for a Christianity in which God is not an afterthought, Christ is the indispensable key to creation, and the unexamined metaphors of modern secularism are never allowed to drown out the radical language of the Gospel."

— David C. Steinmetz, Kearns Distinguished Professor Emeritus, Duke Divinity School

"What would it sound like if Balaam's ass channeled G. K. Chesterton for hipster Christians and cool skeptics? It would sound something like Tyler Blanski in *When Donkeys Talk*. If sound philosophy in a breezy, chatty style is your cup of tea, you will want to drink deeply from this book."

— Donald T. Williams, PhD, author of *Stars Through the Clouds, Reflections from Plato's Cave,* and *Inklings of Reality*

"Tyler Blanski here works a deep magic in bringing to vivid life the riches of the sacramental vision."

— Rodney Clapp, author of *Tortured Wonders: Spirituality for People, Not Angels*

"We are living under a spell, says Tyler Blanski, a spell called Atomland, the land of appearances, where all the mystery, miracle, and magic have been drained out of life. In *When Donkeys Talk* Tyler introduces us to another spell, a spell of deeper magic that has the power to wake us from our slumber, freeing us to experience a more profound and captivating reality than anything we have experienced before. Take the enchanted journey with him; you may never be the same again."

— Jim Belcher, author of *Deep Church*

"It takes a gifted writer like Tyler Blanski not only to get away with using a talking donkey as invitation to a 'holy renaissance,' but also to make it seem like the best invitation you've gotten in years."

— Amy Lyles Wilson, Earlham School of Religion

"*When Donkeys Talk* is a call for a new Reformation from one of a generation falling in love again with Classical Christianity. Witty, winsome, unapologetically faithful, Tyler Blanski offers a new turn on Christian apologetics."

— The Rev. Steven A. Peay, PhD, Associate Dean
for Academic Affairs, Associate Professor of
Homiletics and Church History, Nashotah House

"Who knew that you could present powerful Christian apologetics with tongue firmly in cheek? Tyler Blanski's book does just what St. Augustine says our rhetoric should do: he informs, he persuades, and he delights."

— David Bartlett, Professor Emeritus,
Columbia Theological Seminary and Yale Divinity School

"Honest, whimsical, deeply theological, at times even comical and very accessible. Tyler is a contemporary apologist of an unusual sort, in an era that claims that apologetics are dead. Not so! In the light of the Gospel he helps us think about and call to account many issues at play in today's culture; casting a vision for a different, God-filled way of living."

> —The Rev. Jack Gabig, PhD, Associate Professor of Practical Theology, Nashotah House Theological Seminary; Chair of the Catechesis Task Force, Anglican Church in North America

"In equal measure charming and mischievous, *When Donkeys Talk* invites us to engage a Christian world more real than our constructs of it, and Tyler Blanski shows himself a winsome voice yearning hopefully for a Christian renaissance."

> —Garwood P. Anderson, Professor of New Testament and Greek, Nashotah House Theological Seminary

"Teachers are especially proud when their pupils write good books. *When Donkeys Talk* is now the second time Tyler Blanski has made me especially proud. His latest book is clear, clever, articulate, insightful, and memorable. It is classical spirituality dressed in modern garments and spoken in accessible language. In short, it's very, very good."

> —Dr. Michael Bauman, Professor of Theology and Culture, Hillsdale College; Scholar in Residence, Summit Semester, Summit Ministries

When Donkeys Talk

A Quest to Rediscover
the Mystery and Wonder of Christianity

Tyler Blanski

ZONDERVAN®

ZONDERVAN.com/

We want to h ⬛ 3064513099387 ⬛ ⬛ts about this
book to u ⬛ ⬛ hank you.

ZONDERVAN

When Donkeys Talk
Copyright © 2012 by Tyler Blanski

This title is also available as a Zondervan ebook. Visit www.zondervan.com/ebooks.

This title is also available in a Zondervan audio edition. Visit www.zondervan.fm.

Requests for information should be addressed to:
Zondervan, *Grand Rapids, Michigan 49530*

Library of Congress Cataloging-in-Publication Data

Blanski, Tyler.
    When donkeys talk : a quest to rediscover the mystery and wonder of Christianity /
Tyler Blanski.
      p.   cm.
      Includes bibliographical references.
      ISBN 978-0-310-33498-9 (softcover)
      1. Christianity—Miscellanea. I. Title.
  BR123.B573—2013
  230—dc23   2012034382

Cover design: Faceout Studio
Cover illustration: Shutterstock®
Interior design: Michelle Espinoza

Printed in the United States of America

---

12 13 14 15 16 17 18 19 /DCI/ 24 23 22 21 20 19 18 17 16 15 14 13 12 11 10 9 8 7 6 5 4 3 2 1

For my dear friend, Michael Ward

"This was the very reason you were brought to Narnia,
that by knowing me here for a little, you may know me better there."

How much happier you would be,
how much more of you there would be,
if the hammer of a higher God
could smash your small cosmos.

—G. K. Chesterton, *Orthodoxy*

Contents

Foreword

I would like to introduce Tyler Blanski's wonderful new book *When Donkeys Talk* by first telling a bit about my own family. Please have patience with this foreword. It will make sense in the end.

My grandfather, Juan Melquiades Ortega, died in 1991, just a couple months shy of his 102nd birthday. He was a Christian man whose quiet devotion to God found expression in the unlikely combination of gifts bestowed on him by the Creator — farming, weaving, storytelling, and singing.

My grandfather's farm tied him to the earth — its unpredictable seasons, the needs of his family, the phases of the moon.

His magnificent weavings (two of which belong to the Smithsonian Institution) were the products of slow, painstaking processes — the shearing of sheep, the spinning of wool, vats of dye.

The stories my grandfather told us were about long-gone distant relatives who herded sheep in Colorado and Gypsies who camped at the edge of town in the 1930s, selling their wares — potions and pots. My favorite story was about an old witch who could turn herself into a coyote. She tried to trick some cousins of mine who were on their way to a dance. One of the cousins was named Juan, a name considered to possess spiritual power over dark forces. Juan drew a circle in the dirt around the witch and called out the names "Jesús, María y José!" and the witch was trapped in the circle, unable to do any harm to my cousins.

These stories grounded us in our history and the past, yet they set our imaginations free to wander the llanos and riverbeds of northern New Mexico for ourselves. They still have that same magic all these years later.

Lastly, it was the gift of song that connected my grandfather to the transcendent God he worshiped through the work of his hands. On hot summer nights he sang under the canopy of stars while he irrigated rows of chile, corn, tobacco, and melons—his voice muted by the soft earth, water, and the rhythm of a spade.

A year after my grandfather's death, I wrote a song called "Mi Abuelito" that memorializes much of what I have described above. I frequently perform it in concerts to this day. Though it's a crowd favorite, I have all too often been called to task for penning a lyric that makes no specific mention of God. I've given up arguing about it. In my mind, it's one of my most God-filled songs. Herein lies my great enthusiasm for *When Donkeys Talk*—a terrific book by a bearded young Anglican from Minneapolis, of all places.

Tyler Blanski adores Jesus and downright loves Christianity, the historical kind. He holds his faith up like a flaming torch in the face of scientism and secularism. His book is a wild and joyous ride through coffee houses, campsites, Christmas tree lots, medieval history, and the vast expanse of the starry universe. All these places come together and find their meaning in the incarnation of Christ. In the same beautiful way, my grandfather's farm, his stories, songs, and woolen blankets find their meaning in the Bethlehem manger where God became flesh.

Tyler and I have texted and emailed back and forth these last few months in anticipation of his book release. He often begins his texts with "Hello Fernando. Christ is among us!" *When Donkeys Talk* is filled with that proclamation. Christ is among us when we are sick in bed with a cold (as I am now), or when we drive to work, or tell our kids a story at night. Though we may not be cognizant of it, we are participants in an eternal song that is being sung by all creation, joined by all the saints who have gone before us and all the heavenly host who are gathered before God's throne. Together we are proclaiming, "Christ is among us!"

Juan Fernando Ortega
October 30, 2012

Acknowledgments

Thank you to my wife, Brittany.

Thank you, Petersons, Michael Ward, Ivan, Father Peay, and the professors of Nashotah House.

Thank you to my editors, Carolyn McCready, Andy Meisenheimer, and Jim Ruark.

Thank you, Tom Dean and Jess Secord.

Thank you, Fernando Ortega.

Mom and Dad—thank you.

Part 1

A Crazy-Ass Theory

In Which donkeys can talk and Christianity is an old-growth forest. Stephen the Philistine is introduced. So are a crazy-ass theory and the holy trinity of breakfast. The incarnation has comprehensive implications for the universe and for us. If donkeys can talk, so can the stars and our calendars, our very lives. We do not need a revival; we need a holy renaissance. But the path through Christendom is old and dangerous, and careful reconnoitering is necessary.

Behold, thy king cometh unto thee;
  he is just, and having salvation;
lowly, and riding upon an ass,
  even upon a colt, the foal of an ass.

  —Zechariah 9:9 ASV

I shall not count it dishonorable to ride on such a beast, for I remember reading that when good old Silenus, the tutor of the merry god of laughter, rode into the city of the hundred gates, he did so, much to his satisfaction, on a handsome ass.

  —Cervantes, *Don Quixote*

Chapter 1

Holy Pilgrimage

f I were to tell you that I had a talking donkey, you would probably chuckle and pour another drink. If I were to insist that I was entirely serious, you would probably back away slowly and, with no masked alarm, look for the nearest exit. Nothing ruins a good party like a story about a miracle. "It was a trick of the nerves, an illusion," those who dared to hang around would counsel, surveying me with concerned puppy eyes. "Have you taken your medication?" I do not have a donkey, but if I did, I would want it to be a talking donkey.

It all started with eggs, hash browns, and bacon — the holy trinity of breakfast. Sitting at a local bar in the a.m., quaffing down cheap coffee, eavesdropping the gossip about a politician at a nearby table, I heard a fellow omnivore exclaim, "Who sent her crazy ass to Congress?" The phrase caught my attention because growing up I was a skateboarder who wore long chains that jingled and had long hair that was greasy, and my friends would remark, "That's some crazy-ass hair, man." *Crazy ass* connotes something loony — with a comedic, cool, or half-baked twist. I looked up from my thick-cut smoky strips and saw the Democratic donkey emblazoned on a diner's shirt, and that's when it all came together. Crazy. Ass. The donkey. The Holy

Trinity. I remembered the Bible story of Balaam and his crazy ass, and in a moment of rare epiphany, I realized I had never taken that story seriously. In fact, I had never taken most of the Bible that seriously. I had somehow turned the historic stories of God-on-earth into "life lessons," as if Christianity were a kind of therapy. I had turned a blind eye to the possibility that the Bible stories are not only life-rattling, but historically and ontologically true—Christianity not as a personal belief but a public fact.

In the fourth book of the Torah, Numbers, a book written long before Jesus Christ was born, there is a story about a pagan named Balaam. Back then paganism was the popular science. Gods, not forces or principles, were why rocks fell, ocean tides swelled, and crops grew. Everyone believed in gods, even the "secular" Gentiles, sometimes even the Jews. From the Hebrew perspective, it could be said that to be "secular" was to be non-Jewish: though the Gentiles believed in gods, they did not believe in the one true God. So it is strange that this Gentile, Balaam, would be a prophet. Though he was a pagan, Balaam believed in the one true God.[1]

According to legend, Balaam had the gift of knowing the exact moment of God's anger—he was a superprophet, a soothsayer, and God spoke to him in dreams and visions. Scripture says, "The LORD put a word in Balaam's mouth" (Num. 23:5 KJV).[2] His very name means "to swallow."[3] The Israelites had just spent forty years wandering in the desert and were about to cross the Jordan River into the green land of Canaan. They had already begun conquering its inhabitants, and the king of Moab was afraid he was next in line on the Israelite knock-off list. He sent for the prophet Balaam, "the swallower of people," to rain down curses on the Israelites.[4] And so Balaam saddled his ass, the donkey he had ridden since he was a boy, and waddled his way to the king of Moab.

But God took issue with Balaam's plans to curse his chosen people. On his journey, an angel of the Lord appeared before Balaam and his ass and unsheathed a sword to block their path. Balaam couldn't see the angel at first, but the ass could. Much to the amusement of Balaam's entourage, the terrified beast scampered into the byway fields carrying the bouncing Balaam with it. Embarrassed, Balaam whisked the donkey back onto the path only to be flung against a wall further down the road when the angel appeared a second time. His feet bruised and his face rouged, Balaam whaled on the ass with a stick. As they inched along, the angel appeared a third time and frightened Balaam's donkey to the point of paralysis (donkeys are very stubborn — unlike horses, you can't cajole a donkey to do anything that is not in its best interest). Outraged, Balaam beat the ass with his stick yet again, or, as the King James Version puts it, "he smote the ass with a staff" (Num. 22:27).

The Lord then made the donkey speak. "What have I done? This is the third time you've beaten me!" Balaam answered, "You have made a fool of me! If I had a sword with me, I'd kill you!" But the donkey retorted, "Am I not still the ass which you have ridden since you were a boy? Have I ever taken such a liberty with you before?" And then the Lord opened Balaam's eyes and he saw the angel standing there with his sword drawn. Terrified, Balaam fell flat on his face, and the angel told him he could continue his journey to the king of Moab, but he must not curse the Israelites; rather, he must bless them. And, as the story unfolds, we see that his prayers of blessing actually changed what happened to the Israelites.

This is in more senses than one a crazy-ass story. Here we see an ass, well known for its dopiness and obstinacy, illustrating more spiritual insight than the great pagan prophet of Mesopotamia.[5] A "dumb ass speaking with [a] man's voice," is how the King James Version phrases it (2 Peter 2:16), saving the life of its master, a soothsayer who voices omens and auguries from God. Though the tale is ironic and funny, it is deadly serious. God, it would seem, can use anyone—from a heathen to an ass—to accomplish his will.[6] Sadly, like Balaam, we often go blundering on our way, blind to the warnings of God until he has to use "asses" to stop us. But the love of God is more real than the law of gravity. Angels are everywhere. Any donkey could be a talking donkey. We just need God to open our eyes as he did Balaam's. And so as a Christian, and Christians believe in a lot of weird things,[7] this story has become my coat of arms for what I believe to be one of today's most important battles: our (mostly quiet) presuppositions about what to expect from Christendom.

"Christendom" is God's kingdom expanding through that large, loose communion of saints, the church, whom Cyprian calls "the bright army of the soldiers of Christ."[8] Saint Ambrose calls it "God's kingdom, which is the church."[9] To become a Christian is to become a part of a loose and sympathetic clump of people from different walks of life and different age groups but all experiencing the same weather, same hardships, same topography, same eccentric impulse to follow Jesus. It's a personality cult really. This Jesus, this Christ, this "luminous Nazarene," as Einstein called him, is a personality with whom to reckon. These Christ-followers say Jesus the Christ (Greek for "Anointed One") is fully human and fully God and that he has broken into our world, our time. They say you can know him and be known by him and be loved by him and that his love can transform your life—this very day, this very moment. They have been saying this for millennia. Generation after generation of creative artists and linear left-brainers alike are drawn by tractor beam to his wisdom, his moxie, his unfathomable love. And they are in awe of him. They say the God of history, the God of the ages, has broken into their lives and started a renovation of the human heart. They say he changes everything—relationships, food and drink, history, even the unseen mysteries of space and time.

Nonetheless, some of my Christian friends (I used to be one of them) do not like Balaam's crazy-ass story. They enjoy the other donkey stories, like the one in which a donkey blinks at the newborn baby Jesus, or in which Abraham loads up his donkey as he heads off to sacrifice his son Isaac, or the one in which Jesus hoofs it into Jerusalem on the back of a donkey to be sacrificed for the world while crowds shout "Hosanna!" In these stories, at least, this domesticated hoofed mammal of the horse family with long ears and a braying call is just a normal, old donkey.

But I'm curious: if I can believe in Jesus (that immaculately fertilized ovum), why can't I believe in talking donkeys? Is not my whole presupposition that the world is miraculous? "Why should any of you consider it incredible that God raises the dead?" asked Paul, as if it happens all the time (Acts 26:8). Few forget, having read it once, how God spoke to Moses "in flames of fire from within a bush" (Ex. 3:2). Fewer still can ignore how in Matthew 26:75 Jesus employed a rooster to communicate to his disciple Peter. Or what about the poetry of the war-horse in Job 39:25, who "at the blast of the trumpet ... snorts, 'Aha!'" Or what about when Moses parted the Red Sea (Ex. 14:21–22) or when Joshua commanded the sun to pause in the sky, and it really did (Josh. 10:12–13). If I already believe that God himself was tortured to death and then rose from the dead, and that the actual *blood* of Jesus has the power to forgive sins, why would I doubt for a moment that Elijah called down fire from heaven to burn up a sacrifice (1 Kings 18:36–39)?

I used to tell myself, "Christianity is not miraculous; Christianity is safe." I did not want a God who was bigger than me, who would shake things up. Safe is what I wanted, and sadly, safe is what I got. But lately I have longed for something more than a Christianity that looks like the advertisements and suburbs of the twentieth century. I want to discover the God who really lives and breathes, the God who changes everything about what it means to be human. Christianity is not safe. It opens up a world brimming with hellfire and judgment, damnation and salvation, real evil and real good, and most of all real love, the kind of love you have elsewhere known only in faint imitations and foretastes. Christendom (for it really is just that, the Christian *world*) is full of talking donkeys, burning bushes, floods, talking serpents, crowing roosters, and disastrous apples that, if bitten, will steal your immortality.

It is full of deep magic.

In the story of Don Quixote and Sancho Panza, this ordinary guy decides to don an old suit of armor and set out on a knight-errant in search of adventure. He dubs his buddy Sancho a squire. The two of them embark on elaborate horseback quests that they think are real, even though they are not. They attack windmills that they think are ferocious giants.

I want to invite you to join me on what might turn out to be a not-so-wild goose chase. Because there is, after all, something rather ferocious and giantlike about windmills, don't you think? I want to saddle a donkey and clip-clop through "the Olde World." We're looking for relics of a bygone era—an era when donkeys talked and stars shone bright and saints weren't naysayers. We're hoofing it to church and to the old books. Like the Christians of yore, we want to live a life in God's presence. We want to dust off what C. S. Lewis called "the discarded image" and Owen Barfield called "that discarded garment."[10] We want to wake up to the possibility that Jesus could communicate to us by way of donkey—or dog or cat or rubber ducky. Our mission will be to wake up, to become enchanted. I'll leave it to you to decide if anything we discover is worthwhile—and you can also decide who of us is the handsome knight and who's the stout squire.

And so what you are holding is an invitation to go on a holy pilgrimage. It's a treasure map. And it will lead you through some of the most beautiful and dangerous terrain in Christianity, lands long forgotten or neglected, lands it will take a holy renaissance to rediscover. If I had to capture what I'm looking for with a word, I would call it *belief*, the kind of belief that invites me to live the childlike faith Jesus says is the entry door of his house, the kingdom of heaven (Mark 10:15).

Chapter 2

In Search of Magic

To begin my pilgrimage, I marched across the street to see my neighbor, Stephen the Philistine, an old college buddy of mine. His height, his amazingly voluminous mustache, and his brilliant blue eyes lend him a handsome but fierce charm. He's called Stephen the Philistine because, even though he knows more about Christianity than most Christians, he just doesn't believe. He will not stand hypocrisy. He also loves women and adventure and Bombay Sapphire gin. Christianity has all of this, I've told him—just not the way he wants it. Anyway, I stomped across the street to announce to Stephen the Philistine that I was writing a Christian book about my crazy-ass theory.

"I love it when people say ridiculous things," he said, looking at me like I had just toddled out of the church nursery.

"Yeah?" I asked, feeling mildly heartened.

"Sure," he said, waving his hand. "But Christians don't. Your silly book will ruin you."

I gulped. "Well, at least decapitations and drownings and burnings at the stake are no longer church practice."

"Right," said Stephen, comfortingly. His eyes looked bluer. "And the U.S. Constitution and Bill of Rights are on your side too."

"Mind if I have some of your gin?" I asked.

"Not at all," Stephen replied, and fixed me a strong Christian drink.

Despite the comforting words of an old friend, I walked back across the street to my apartment, and worry swept over me like a cloud. I called Stephen on my cell phone.

"Yeah," Stephen said in a clipped tone.

"What if people think I'm a heretic?"

"Tyler, Christians *always* get angry when you challenge their stereotypes about God and magic and science. Don't worry. Even if we actually lived in medieval times and still shouted at one another names like "heretic," folks couldn't really call you a heretic—and you couldn't really call them heretics for disagreeing with you either."

"Why?" I asked.

"Because, as far as I can tell, no part of your crazy-ass theory calls into question or contradicts the orthodoxy of the Nicene Creed—or the Apostles' Creed, or the creed of Saint Athanasius. You're the theologian. You should know this."

I nodded, but Stephen, of course, cannot hear nods. He continued into the silence: "Regardless of whether anybody agrees with you or not, just be grateful to have them as your travel companions. I'll be happy to sign the naysayers up for a jousting match—you know, the kind where noble knights on horses best one another with lances. Or we could all just sit and talk over a friar's red ale."

I weakly laughed.

Greatly cheered by Stephen the Philistine's words, I threw my phone on the couch and wrote down a few questions: What does it mean to live in a world where donkeys can talk? What does it mean to be a God-*created* man or woman? Where do we belong in the universe? What does it mean that God not only reveals himself through words but actually became human, incarnate? What are Christians doing, exactly, when they get baptized or receive the Lord's Supper? Is there meaning in the universe that even pagans and secular people can discover, and how do we integrate that with our faith? How did Christians think about church before the age of televisions and cars and corporations?

In a quest to answer questions like these, I am straddling a donkey, holding the reins of a bygone era, perhaps another one to come. I want to discover God's story in reality and on trails overgrown and neglected.

In my early attempts at reconnoitering, I rashly continued to make public my intentions. With much gusto, I announced to family and friends and even my publisher that I would travel Christendom in search of magic. Nearly everyone had some grim admonition or reprimand. The old forest of Christendom is full of peril—bears, feral bobcats, and wild boars, loony hillbillies from the medieval backwoods, lethal old heresies and fables that burrow their way into the brains of hapless hikers and send them off in apostasy and blasphemies. Spooky shapes loom out of a fog thicker than wood smoke. Just read about the visions of Hildegard of Bingen or the impulses of Francis of Assisi, and you'll start to get the idea. Inconceivable things could happen to us out there. Then there is the vexed matter of Saint Denis, who was commissioned to convert the people of Gaul and did such a good job that the local pagans got angry and beheaded him. After something like a blind Easter egg hunt, Denis just picked up his head and kept on preaching. He has become the patron saint for headaches. Then there's Saint Fiacre, who was looking to build a new monastery. The bishop offered him as much land as he could till in one day. He turned up the soil with his staff, toppling trees and crushing huge stones. A suspicious woman told the bishop that Fiacre was using witchcraft. But the bishop recognized that this was the work of the Lord, and Fiacre built his monastery, which, incidentally, barred women. He's the patron saint of gardening and, um, taxi drivers.

And that's the good stuff. Before I got down to any real research, I suffered foreboding stories (always shared with a knowing chuckle and a grin) of woebegone wayfarers who ventured to go on holy pilgrimages only to wake to find themselves bedfellows with pagan astrologers or sharing the same tent with a Germanic tradition for a few confused and colorful moments. Others have gone off hiking the old paths our ancestors trod, only to stumble upon kooks, witches, or horoscope readers. I heard stories of poor pilgrims who suddenly vanished in a heretical haze. Others have wandered into the cloaking mists of what has been called the luminous darkness of God, never to be the same again. It took only a little light reading and almost no imagination for me to envision the same coming true for me.

For example, I recently discovered the only complete novel to survive from the Latin, *The Metamorphoses*. The book influenced Augustine's prose style so much that he nicknamed the ribald tale "The Golden Ass." It tells the story of a poor man who wants to learn magic. He tries to turn himself into a bird but is horrified to discover that he has instead become an ass: "At last, hopelessly surveying myself all over, I was obliged to face the mortifying fact that I had been transformed not into a bird, but into a plain jackass."[1] He then follows a track of adventures much too bawdy and a little too sumptuous to recount here. "Let me tell you, friend Sancho," warned Don Quixote on this matter, "that the life of a knight-errant is subject to a thousand dangers and misfortunes."[2]

But none of the stories I read outdid the stories in the Bible — stories in which God literally stops the earth from spinning, becomes a human being, walks on water, raises Lazarus from the dead, conquers death itself, and promises everlasting life. The more I read, the more determined I became to explore the gothic and the gospel. Despite everything, I decided to plunge irreversibly into the old forest, those days before the so-called Enlightenment's wood chippers. Even though I am no Saint George when it comes to fighting dragons, I hoisted a backpack of library books, tightened my grip on my donkey's reins, and stepped portentously onto the old trail at the edge of the darkening pines.

Chapter 3

A Deepening Conversion

As we shall see in our exploration of the Eucharist in particular, the kingdom of God is extremely nigh. It is my hope that this holy pilgrimage leads us into a deepening conversion. The old forest of Christendom is an invitation to worship—more specifically, to participate in the Eucharist, to affirm yet again that the Man who was born in Bethlehem really was of one substance with the Father, that all things were made by him, and that the mystery of the Word made flesh is made available to us at the Lord's Supper.

Hobbling around a world of talking donkeys plants within a person a new hunger for the body and a new thirst for the blood of the incarnate Word. Enchanted Christianity is a medieval bludgeon to our imaginations. It might even inspire us to again call our bodies "Brother Ass," like Francis of Assisi, that skinny saint who scampered naked through the woods to worship the Lord and love those in need. To him the world was alive with the activity of God. To him, miracles, like electrons, could pop up anywhere, and not every ass was a dumb ass. My one goal for us is to believe like that: to believe better. Belief is not easy, but it shapes our whole lives. For a lot of us, it can seem downright impossible, and it does not help that many churches today are making Christianity confusing.

Growing up I was told that when we go to church, we want to be entertained. This is not true. When we are baptized into the old forests of the kingdom of God, we die to our old self and are raised up into the body of Christ, his church. Thus church is not about our entertainment but about our participation in a shared life of active service in God's kingdom. I was also told that I have a short attention span, and that, in so many words, I am not interested in the intellectual. But in enchanted, covenantal Christendom, we are made in God's image and are endowed not only with an emotional life but with a brain. We are called to be disciples, students, of Jesus. Paul exhorts us to outgrow a diet of "spiritual milk" so that we might become adults in Christ. We should want to learn more about Scripture, theology, the spiritual disciplines, and the story of God's church. We should want to love the Lord our God with all our hearts, souls, bodies, and minds.

Another huge obstacle to traveling historic Christianity is the myth that we do not want religion. The twentieth century thought tradition and history were unfashionable, so it made church look like business school or a shopping outlet. When I went to a church like this, I was persuaded that I did not want to be religious, but that I did want to be "spiritual," "relevant," or even "cool." But what do we expect to receive from a God who can be packaged and presented to us by an entertainment business that carefully markets its product to the moralistic therapeutic deists of the suburbs?[1] Certainly not a real-life encounter with the triune God of the ages, the Creator of the heavens and the earth, the Judge of all humanity, and the Redeemer of the world. *That* God is terrifying. It turns out the saints of yore were badasses (in the "formidable, excellent" sense of the word). They understood that Christianity *is* a religion, that is, embodied, communal faith in action. If I am born again, I can no longer be an individualist or a therapeutic or materialistic deist. I should not want to invent a personal faith of private devotions in my closet at the expense of living actively in the corporate body of Christ's church. The Holy Spirit inside of me cries out for me to *live* my faith in the community of believers. This "lived faith" is religion.

Every church has a liturgy, but not every church has a Christian liturgy. Some have favored the liturgy of the rock concert or the liturgy of the megamall or the liturgy of the corporation. But as Christians, we are called into the liturgy of the church that is not bound by time, the liturgy recognizable to the timeless, worldwide communion of saints. The old school word for this universality, this international, intergenerational community, is catholic (καθολικος, *katholikos*). It's the belief that the church all over the world is the bride of Christ, the beloved of God. When we are the beloved of Jesus, the Word who became flesh and dwelt among us (see John 1:14), we grow increasingly hungry for liturgy. This is because God, who spoke our world into existence, who has chosen words to be his means of special revelation in Scripture, and who demands that we *profess* our faith, is a God of words. "Liturgy" is a believer's role in the Christian community. On Sunday mornings, this role becomes largely one of speaking and listening to words. This reading of Scripture, saying the Creeds, confessing sin, praying the Lord's Prayer, celebrating the Eucharist, and singing songs—and saying and singing corporately—is called "liturgy."

For a lot of us, the beauty of liturgy and holy magic of Christendom might at first be alarming, because we were raised to think that the world is like a toaster oven or that God is some kind of benign first mover. This "disenchantment," to use Max Weber's expression, is witnessed most obviously in our attitude about the Lord's Supper. Many of us have picked up the idea that the Lord's Supper is only a dry custom of eating bread and drinking wine while "thinking about God." It is so much more than a mental gymnastic. If Christianity were the same thing as gnostic dualism, the Holy Eucharist would only be about remembering Jesus. But Christianity is incarnational and miraculous—at least when you're hobbling around on an ass.

Growing up, I was able to dive into different ideas of what Christianity is all about. For my entire childhood, my family went to John Piper's Bethlehem Baptist Church in Minneapolis. It was there my lasting humility before Scripture was first nurtured. I went to a fundamentalist elementary school called Calvin Christian School. But by Junior High, I was attending the local public school instead. Throughout my adolescence, I attended a megachurch in the burbs, Wooddale Church. I lived and breathed Wooddale and even helped start the youth group's worship team. My first sweethearts and closest friends were at the huge church. I eventually grew dreadlocks and worked at an organic foods co-op, and by the time I was seventeen, I was a "covenant participant" at Doug Pagitt's Solomon's Porch, a kind and colorful emergent, postmodern community. Around this time, I started attending the Perpich Center for Arts Education, a unique high school dedicated to the fine arts, to study guitar for my junior and senior years. The school was packed with lesbians and liberals, tattooed thespians and young rappers, and it was there that I started my modest music career. It's more of a hobby, really, but I love writing folk songs, producing albums, and stomping my feet and blowing into my harmonica in the Uptown bars on Friday nights.

Although I beheld much of the behind-the-scenes wonders of the modern art scene, I didn't learn much at the arts high school, and knew it. So I ended up going to, of all places, Hillsdale College in southern Michigan, a school on the opposite end of the political, moral, and educational spectrum. There were only two (alleged) lesbians on campus, and no one seemed to care about fashion or entertainment. At Hillsdale everyone was talking about books and ideas. I had never heard of the liberal arts, and I was shocked to discover in my first semester of a classical education that our Western culture is not something we recently made up. Whether we like it or not, we are the recipients of the Greco-Roman, Judeo-Christian tradition. At Hillsdale I stumbled into the ugliest, tiniest, most ordinary church I had ever seen: Christ's Church, a small Anglican church. It was there I encountered Christendom's beautifully weathered prayers, historic liturgy, and creeds. I witnessed a small band of Christians living together in love in a daily life rooted in Word and sacrament. My faith, I discovered, did not consist of only me and my Bible and my hip church floating alone in outer space. That humble and homely little Anglican church invited me into a faith that was evangelical *and* catholic, ever old *and* ever new, hip but also historic and orthodox. Since I moved back to Minneapolis to paint houses and write books, I have been a member of Church of the Cross, another Anglican church packed with young couples, babies, old people, people of every color and race, teenagers, and midlifers who are in love with Jesus.

I'm not one of those Christians who might as well drive around with a bumper sticker that reads: "We do things our way, and everyone else is an a**hole." I am not bitter about, or in flight from, any of the churches I have known. Together they have shaped my love and devotion to Jesus Christ as Lord in a sometimes broken, sometimes beautiful way. And so this pilgrimage is not about leaving or cleaving with any one particular tradition or denomination. The goal of our journey is not even to retrieve a golden age or to make us become better Baptists or evangelicals or Anglicans. We are on a quest to love God more and to know him better. Exploring Christianity's ancient-future faith breathes new life into our discipleship to Jesus.

Chapter 4

A Restoration Project

We need a holy renaissance. A revival without a renaissance makes only converts — yet to be "Christian" today does not always mean to be Christlike. A renaissance, however, invites us to become disciples of Jesus, to become his lifelong students. I'm just a house-painter from Minneapolis, but I believe the Holy Spirit is stirring a hunger in Christians today for spaces where they can become students — disciples — of Jesus Christ. God's activity on earth, ever old and ever new, is a continuous stream of one salvation story after another, and we are invited to participate in these stories in an intimate way. There actually *is* a great cloud of witnesses (Heb. 12:1). There actually *is* "one universal and apostolic church."[1] And when we were baptized in the name of the Father, Son, and Holy Spirit, we were reborn into this company of saints.

The word *renaissance* usually makes us think of *the* Renaissance, that revival of literature and art in the fourteenth through sixteenth centuries spurred by a renewed interest in the classical models of antiquity. Names like Petrarch, Dante, Boccaccio, and the painter Giotto come to mind — not to mention Raphael, Leonardo da Vinci, and Michelangelo. Music flourished. Art exploded. Literature reached new heights. It is a period that glows in history. People looked to what was good and true from the past and lived it in the present tense.

We are on the cusp of another renaissance—a God renaissance, a holy renaissance—for a renaissance is what happens when new vision and vitality rush into old truths and traditions. People see themselves as part of something bigger and beautiful. They wake up. Minds and hearts come alive. History is changed. We do not need to obsess over what is new or how to "reach the culture." Renaissances don't happen that way. Renaissances happen when people look back to what is good, true, and truly beautiful and then live it in the present tense, live it in their own unique way.

If you don't stir the pot, the soup burns. Renaissances get everyone upset because they stir things up. And so people will either persecute Christians again or become Christians themselves, but they won't be able to yawn and disregard the church because it looks just like the rest of contemporary culture. The church in renaissance strives to be what it is called to be: the light of Christ. Jesus is a battering ram to what it means to be human. Two-thousand-some odd years have not been long enough to fully grasp the implications of the incarnation and the repercussions of the resurrection. The ramifications of what God set in motion on the cross change everything about our world and what it means to be human. Even Balaam and his twitchy-eared donkey are woven into the fabric of Jesus' swaddling clothes. The words of Christ "have in themselves something of dreadful majesty."[2] They change what it means to be human. They are our judgment and hope.

Our galaxy sings of the Lord with a mathematical elegance, an extraordinary subtlety and poetry. It brings me to my knees. It has sometimes even spurred me to dance little jigs in my kitchen, splashing coffee hither and yon. I feel like a boy at the zoo, unashamedly pointing, staring stupidly, calling attention to the donkeys. Throw in some sixteenth-century syntax, ersatz Olde English accents, and even a roasted turkey leg, and you get my crazy-ass theory: the theory that the world is resonate with God, that we can't escape him. We actually live in a "kingdom" where the Lord is *reigning*.

Moses approached the burning bush, the bush ablaze with God, and reverently took off his sandals. For Saint Francis, the whole world was a burning bush ablaze with God, and so out of reverence he never wore sandals.

We, too, should take off our shoes.

Part 2
Atomland

In Which it is suggested that I am not a machine. Britta is introduced, and so is Oliver. Balaam's donkey is brought to the dentist. We explore Atomland, the so-called Enlightenment, and the idea of "saving the appearances." In order to know anything, people have starting points, things they take as givens. For Christians, Jesus is the starting point. He changes everything about what it means to be human. Britta and Tyler have breakfast at the Modern Café.

"So he's going to cut them up," observed Pavel Pertovich; "he has not faith in principles, but he has faith in frogs."

—Ivan Turgenev, *Fathers and Sons*

We treat people, places, and things in accordance with the way we perceive them.

—Wendell Berry, *Life Is a Miracle*

Chapter 5

Taking the Donkey to the Dentist

One brisk autumn evening, I had my good friend Oliver over for frozen pizza. We like to sit in my kitchen and listen to old blues records and drink cheap beer. Oliver has sea-green eyes and stand-up strawberry hair with curls that bounce. He's a computer engineer. Oliver was raised in an orthodox Jewish family but is now an agnostic, and so we always get to talking about real geeky stuff, and we love arguing. Because he knows so much about Hebrew culture, I told him about Balaam and my crazy-ass theory.

He was less than enthused.

"Are you serious?" he asked dubiously, cracking open a canned beer. "Science has proven donkeys can't talk. The universe is governed by fixed laws, Tyler."

"There's no such thing as a 'fixed law,'" I said. Oliver looked at me like I was insane. "What if what we call a 'law' is nothing more than a modernist's metaphor to describe the indescribable?" I asked. "The reason eggs turn into chickens and apples fall from trees is just as mysterious as why Balaam's donkey talked or why Jesus was born of a virgin."

"Um——" Oliver pretended to think for a moment, scratching his urban whiskery face. "No."

"Think about it," I said. "Even though we count on apples falling from trees practically, we can't really claim that they must *always* fall. We can't even really depend on it. We bet on it. We bet on it because of observed repetitions. But it is not a 'law.'"

Oliver put down his beer with authority. "But the law of gravity is an obvious fact, Tyler. It holds the world together. Fixed laws are everywhere. And they prove that miracles are impossible."

"How so?" I asked.

"Well, since you brought it up," he said, "take the Christian myth of the virgin birth. Because of modern science, we know that such a thing could not possibly happen. There must be a male spermatozoon."

It's not every day you hear an old friend say *spermatozoon* with conviction. I thought about what he was saying for a moment.

"But when her fiancé, Joseph, found out she was pregnant, he wanted to call the wedding off," I said.

"Most men would." Oliver nodded vigorously, his curls jiggling like a bowl of red grapes.

"That is, as long he knew that generally a woman cannot have a baby unless she has slept with a man," I said. "That's why at first Joseph wanted to call off the wedding. He didn't just fall off the turnip truck."

"But Joseph *did* just fall off the turnip truck," Oliver retorted, raising his arms in exaggeration. "He *eventually* believed in the virgin birth."

"Yes, but not because he was clueless about where babies come from. Joseph knew babies don't arrive via stork. He just didn't live in a world of unbreakable, fixed 'laws.' For him, the possibility of an apple falling upward was a real possibility. He believed his fiancée's pregnancy was a divine achievement, a miracle, a twist in the expected course of events."

"He probably also believed in elves and orcs and hobbits," Oliver sighed, perhaps annoyed that two at-that-time bachelors were sitting around on a Friday night talking about spermatozoon. The smell of the pizza was beginning to fill the room. "It's not like we're a bunch of Muggles, oblivious to the magic all around us. Modern science has shown there's no such thing as the supernatural," he balked.

"Which of the sciences?" I asked.

"Unless you're a Hufflepuff or a Slytherin," he said blankly, "all of them."

"But science has not demonstrated that there is no supernatural!" I bellowed.

"Why not?" asked Oliver. "No shaman's spell or fast upon a sacred mountain could summon the electromagnetic spectrum. Prophets of the great religions were kept unaware of its existence, not because of a secretive god, but because they lacked the hard-won knowledge of physics. Neurobiology cannot be learned at the feet of a guru. Science is the only viable way to know anything at all."

"Next you'll tell me the mystics would pray better with pocket calculators!" I shouted. The timer went off with a bang. "It is the scientists who are superstitious. It is they who believe in make-believe 'laws' they have never seen. They imagine some dreamy, tender connection between eggs and chickens, between apples leaving trees and apples reaching the ground. But it takes a leap of faith to believe the connection is a 'law.' For all we know, it's magic."

"But science shows that no power could possibly break the fixed laws of the universe. Magic cannot make one and two equal three," replied Oliver. His voice was beginning to rise.

"Of course not," I said, bringing the pizza over to the table. "But believing Elijah could bodily rise up to heaven does not throw into doubt one and two making three. Scientists talk about birth and death and rivers flowing downstream as if these things are as obvious and *necessary* as one and two making three. But they are not."

"It's just not rational," interjected Oliver.

"But it *is* rational," I insisted. "True, 'facts' usually repeat themselves. But how we explain these repetitions is left to reason. And reason does not exclude the possibility that an apple could fall upward or that a virgin could give birth to a son. Imagining a connection between spermatozoon and a baby and calling it a 'law of nature' does not make it *necessary*. Christians believe in miracles, but they do not live in a world of unproven axioms. They live in history, a story of creation, fall, redemption, and consummation."

Oliver looked at me over our cooling pizza like I was not making any sense. So I tried to explain my thinking from another angle. "If you have five dollars on your dresser, does arithmetic guarantee you'll have five dollars there tomorrow?" I asked.

"Absolutely," said Oliver imperiously. "Unless my roommate steals it."

"So," I said, lifting slices of pizza onto our plates. "The laws of arithmetic tell us how much money will be on your dresser *as long as* there is no outside interference, no burglar roommate to break the laws of decency?"

"Of course," replied Oliver, exasperated and unfolding a napkin.

"And so, an ovum cannot be fertilized without a spermatozoon — unless there's been outside interference, a 'divine burglar roommate,' in a manner of speaking. Reason would allow for this possibility regardless of an appeal to the mere repetition of physical facts."

Oliver paused. "The whole thing just brushes me the wrong way," he huffed.

"Please forgive me," I said with a smile, shoving a plate toward him. "I did not realize you were covered in fur."

We laughed and ate a lot of pizza. We decided not to talk about miracles — or spermatozoon, for that matter — again that night. Instead, we stuck to records and beer.[1]

Long after Oliver left, I stood at the sink washing a week's worth of dishes and thinking. Christianity presents a very different story than secularism. "Jesus Christ — who, as it turns out, was born of a virgin, cheated death, and rose bodily into the heavens — can now be eaten in the form of a cracker," writes the pop scientist Sam Harris, baffled by the miraculous.[2] Skeptics take it in good faith that imaginary "laws" hold things together and that nothing can break them. But by their kind of reasoning, they might as well believe magic is the key to the universe.

I could not help but wonder: is a talking donkey a divine portent or a dental problem? Everything about our modern presuppositions is pitted against the possibility of miracles. If Balaam were a modern scientist and he heard his donkey talk, he would probably study the donkey's vocal cords. He would speculate as to whether they were physically capable of producing human sounds, and if so, how the folds of membranous tissue that project inward from the sides of the larynx to form a slit across the glottis in the throat align with the donkey's airstream so that their edges vibrate to produce the phenomenon we call "voice."

But if Balaam were a poet, and if he heard his donkey talk, he would simply *listen*. He would weigh the meaning of the donkey's words. He would consider what action these words might require of him. Both Balaam the scientist and Balaam the poet experience the same miracle. Both are correct in their observations. But they receive entirely *different* information. They live grossly contradicting stories. One blesses the Israelites, while the other takes the donkey to the dentist.

Chapter 6

Christendom and Atomland

People in Christendom live a different story than people in "Atomland," a world inhabited by materialists who believe only atoms, the laws of physics, and the sheer physical world exist. Nothing is wrong with science or the scientific method, but something is wrong with believing the whole universe consists only of colorful, interlocking plastic bricks and an accompanying array of gears, mini-figures, and various gadgets, as if the world were made of Legos. These interlocking bricks, some say, are the building blocks of everything, even love, even the idea of God. Richard Dawkins notices that, statistically, people of faith inherit faith from their parents, and concludes that although "soaring cathedrals, stirring music, moving stories and parables, help a bit . . . your religion is the accident of birth." He concludes that religion really must be based on "epidemiology, not evidence."[1] You are nothing but a random by-product of time and chance.

Sometimes I wonder if a spell has been cast over the modern empirical skyline. So many people trust in statistics, or in fashion, or even in the papier-mâché pragmatic. Some friends of mine have gone so far as to say that love is an adaptation for the survival of the species. I think the spell was first cast in the twelfth century when Averroës insisted on reason being somehow *opposed* to revelation, and eventually came to fruition in the seventeenth century when philosophers like Descartes, Locke, Newton, and Bacon shook their fairy godmother wands and said, in so many words, "The world is now a machine." Slowly we began to see ourselves as objects capable of stepping out of our environment so that we might poke it, manipulate it, and control it. No longer creatures (*creaturae*) created by a Creator, we were free to become autonomous beings capable of forging everything around us into an extension of our own will. Finally, man could crawl out of the mud from which he was made and become godlike.

It took four hundred years, but the spell has now taken full effect. Have you ever gotten that angry feeling when your computer freezes or the plumbing gets clogged or the free Wi-Fi at the local coffee shop isn't working? It's more than an angry feeling. I have been genuinely enraged, infuriated, when my cell phone malfunctions. One would think I would get infuriated about injustice or persecution, but instead I lose it over a slow Internet connection. My laptop no longer exists to keep my life running smoothly; it offends my self-absorption. My illusion of mastery over the world, my delusion of omnipotence, is shattered. When we peel back the layers to expose the raw pulse of what's really going on in those moments of anger—when the fridge breaks or the sink is inexplicably clogged—we might find that the shift in perspective that started with what historical shoptalk calls the "Enlightenment" was no less than the forging of a golden calf.

The modern era said, "I decide what is reality," and the postmodern era took this individualism to the umpteenth degree. The relativism so often associated with postmodernism is really a kind of hypermodernism. It's the ideology of Atomland: "Nature is dead. Therefore meaning is whatever I read into it, and truth is whatever I want it to be." Do this long enough and we begin to feel like gods. We want trophies for simply showing up wearing soccer shorts.

The modern age sought mastery by means of control and openly celebrated the machine for raising us up out of the mud. Today we have gone one step further—we've lived with machines so long we really believe we have transcended our creatureliness. Have you noticed how everything from a toaster oven to an iPod is now designed to look like it is not a machine? All the inner workings, the "guts," are hidden from view. You couldn't take a microwave apart if you wanted to. The spell has become fully cast: we have mastery without having to acknowledge how. Is it any wonder we are livid when the electricity goes out or when we need to call the plumber? Our sense of autonomy and lordship is jeopardized, exposing a frightened, muddy, dependent, social and mortal *creaturae*.

Under the shadow of Atomland, there are no miracles, because no one looks for them. Even if a donkey talked to you in Shakespearean English, you would not believe it happened. What will we do at midnight when our glass slippers vanish and our carriages turn back into pumpkins? Nothing is wrong with machines or technology. But something is wrong with the Atomland, the make-believe world where creation is one big Godless mechanical accretion. It scoffs at religion while being itself a religion—scientism, the radical belief in the power of scientific knowledge and technique to save humanity.

Many contemporary thinkers forget that, although sometimes helpful, to describe the universe as a machine is not to proclaim a deep truth but to employ a broken metaphor hammered out on the jumpy and stubborn typewriters of the modern era.[2] The paradox of biochemistry, the chemistry of life, is that it cannot define life. It can hardly study life. We must kill a cell before we can pick it apart. "It is typical of the mechanistic moderns," said G. K. Chesterton, "that, even when they try to imagine a live thing, they can only think of a mechanical metaphor from a dead thing."[3]

As I am only on a donkey, it is very possible that I do not sit high enough to be convinced that we are nothing but a cloud of atoms. But as far as I can tell, people make machines; they are not themselves machines. The human body is not a computer or a wind-up toy. It is more than a complex composition of atoms, or interconnecting blocks. From one perspective, "the three-pound human brain,"[4] might work *like* a machine; but this does not mean it *is* a machine. In the face of ethics, great art, or human suffering, pointing out that humans have atoms is trivial. It's like saying that music is a violin on a stand while ignoring the violinist and the composer. "Who could understand music only from analysis of the composition of the instruments of an orchestra?" asks Erwin Chargaff. "The news that all trombones are made of brass is trivial when measured against the immensity of the musical universe. Saint Cecilia may have blown sweetly on a trumpet of glass."[5] Which is truer: the music or the instruments? Or are the two inseparably interlocked?

Or, to use a different metaphor: when people in Atomland see kids playing with Legos, the only reality they acknowledge is the acrylonitrile butadiene styrene plastic the Lego bricks are made of and how these pieces interlock to an exacting degree of precision. They overlook the kids and the fact that the kids are building a castle with noble knights and fair ladies and engaging in battles against dangerous dragons. Which is more real: the kids and the story or the Legos?

Chapter 7

Saving the Appearances

In a make-believe world made only of Legos, people begin to think with pop scientist Sam Harris that religion is a mental illness and that theology is nothing more than a branch of human ignorance.[1] According to theoretical physicist Stephen Hawking, believing the brain is a computer will cure people of religion. In an interview, Hawking proclaimed this new mythology: "I regard the brain as a computer which will stop working when its components fail. There is no heaven or afterlife for broken down computers; that is a fairy story for people afraid of the dark."[2] Ethologist Richard Dawkins agrees, writing, "There is no spirit-driven life force, no throbbing, heaving, pullulating, protoplasmic, mystic jelly. Life is just bytes and bytes and bytes of digital information."[3]

Indeed, the widely acclaimed, best-selling author and biologist Edward Wilson says babies are "marvelous robots."[4] He suggests in his *On Human Nature* (a strange title to issue forth from the laboratory) that the brain is a purely biological machine of ten billion nerve cells, a device for survival and reproduction. People are nothing more than "extremely complicated machines," and "the brain is a machine."[5] What we call thinking is really just chemical and electrical reactions. We are the product of our own molecular architecture, which automatically steers our ethics, which happens to be the only thing that distinguishes us from electronic computers. Chance and environmental necessity created the species. God is our original idea produced by the genetic evolution of nervous and sensory tissues, an idea that ultimately finds origin in quarks and electron shells. Thus, "beliefs are really enabling mechanisms for survival."[6]

The word that does all the muscle work for thinkers in Atomland is *really*. When someone says *a* is really *b*, the "really" is shorthand for "Although I can neither prove it nor disprove it, you should listen to me because I have a secret knowledge (γνωσις, *gnosis*)." It is like saying, "If the emperor is walking around naked, he is *really* wearing invisible clothes. The emperor is naked. Therefore his clothes are invisible." We might not be able to logically refute the belief in invisible clothes, but we can know a lot about the kind of people who wear them. The method of pop scientists tends to settle by dictum ideas that remain open to question and to variation, even from inside the community of scientists. Empirical testing has not in the least demonstrated that there really is no God, that ethics really is just an adaptation for the survival of the species, and that we are really just machines. These are the guesswork explanations of a philosophy that begins with the assumption that there is no God.

Although I've read Wilson's words many times, I can see them as nothing but an oxymoron: "The human mind evolved to believe in the gods. It did not evolve to believe in biology."[7] He goes on to explain that belief in God evolved because it offers an adaptive advantage but that belief in biology did *not* evolve because it is "a product of the modern age."[8] He speculates with missionary zeal that freedom is a self-delusion[9] but also says that it is a helpful illusion because it gives our species an adaptive edge.[10] "We can be proud as a species because, having discovered that we are alone, we owe the gods very little."[11] The farmer-poet Wendell Berry bravely observes of this proud and utterly unscientific claim, "This would be a noble blasphemy, like that of Job's wife, if the empiricist or Mr. Wilson believed in the gods, but neither one of them does. It is only a weary little cliché of a too familiar 'scientific' iconoclasm — hubris without a bang."[12]

From Wilson to Hawking, from Harris to Dawkins and the late Christopher Hitchens, the prophets of Atomland cloak their philosophies in the invisible garments of science. Their "emperor wears no clothes" platitudes are mouthed in classrooms, propaganda, and contemporary journalism. Before the silvered tureen of these writers' intellectual snobbery, ordinary folks with legitimate doubts and honest questions fall like grouse to the gun. The good-natured and nonscholarly public suffers them gladly. Their books give us a good snapshot into the kinds of unscientific assumptions scientists expect us to accept in good faith.

You really cannot walk down the street without bumping into someone of Wilson's ilk or a fan. I'm not kidding — after I walked the four blocks from my Uptown apartment to my favorite Minneapolis used bookstore to purchase Wilson's *On Human Nature*, I stepped into a nearby coffeehouse. Within minutes an attractive girl with very long and luxurious dreadlocks sat down beside me and exclaimed, "I love that book. Wilson is my hero. What do you think of him?" I said I thought he was a good writer who had a lot to say but that I was not too sure of his presuppositions. "Huh," she said, casting a privately thoughtful glance at my near medieval beard, instantly more interested in her espresso than me. We didn't say another word. It was as if someone drew a curtain. I was sad but a little relieved to be spared the possibility of asking such a pretty lady out only to unearth this news later, over a candlelit dinner perhaps:

· "Um, you believe in whom?" she would ask in honest surprise, her gorgeous dreads spilling out of her bandana.

"Jesus," I would repeat, staring into her blue eyes. The restaurant would become suddenly quiet.

"But, like, haven't you heard of *biology*?"

"But of course."

She would nod primly and cross her alabaster arms. Then, with a flood of pity, she would lean over: "Actually, did you know the brain is really an *appliance*?" she'd whisper, inviting me to share her amazement. "It's even fueled by biochemicals and capable of mass-producing ideas as big as God, you know." When donkeys are happy, they prick up their ears; when they are scared or nervous, their ears tuck down, like Eeyore in Winnie-the-Pooh. If you were stealing furtive glances at me and my hot date, and if I had donkey ears, I don't know what state they would be in. One hopes you'd find them to be upright and curious ears, while I blinking dreamily would ask, "Is that all the brain is?"

This is the thing. Before the modern era, people were conscious that their theories about how the world works were just that: theories. They called their data "phenomena," which to them meant something like what we mean by the word *appearances*. The phrase that dominated astronomy in the Middle Ages was "to save the appearances."[13] A scientific model was valued because it was convenient or practical, not because it was what we today would call a fact. The idea was to work with the explanatory models or paradigms best capable of "saving the phenomena" (σώζειν τά φαινομένη, *sozein ta phainomena*). An astronomer's hypothesis was an arrangement, a prop, for saving the appearances. "Things *appear* to be this way," he would say. "They *seem* to be thus and such; they *give the impression* of being so." The scientists in the sixteenth century, who also happened to be bishops, did not disagree with Galileo for his use of the telescope or his spotting Jupiter's moons. They disagreed with his theory of a *theory*. Galileo believed a theory is not a theory, but a fact. His hypotheses did not "save the appearances," but claimed to state truth.[14]

The notion that the models and stories we write to explain the phenomena are actually deep truths was codified in the so-called Enlightenment of the seventeenth century and has since become unquestioned. Watching someone try to understand that the "law of gravity" is a man-made metaphor to describe the inexplicable is like watching someone wrestle a demon off his shoulders. People actually think "science" exists independent of or outside of the human narrative, the way a medieval thinker would think of God. Thus scientists can say things about evolving to believe in God, not biology.[15] Christians believe created human beings lack any goal apart from Christ. The Trinity, therefore, is the key to human nature. But scientists under the spell of Atomland believe that biology is the key to human nature.[16] Phenomena are no longer acknowledged as man-made models, but as established facts. "When the nature and limitations of artificial images are forgotten," writes Barfield, "they become idols."[17]

The longer we explore the differences between Atomland and Christendom, the more we discover these outlooks on reality are in direct opposition to one another. One is the City of God, the other is the City of Man.[18] Each city asks different questions. Physicist Paul

Dirac gives this answer to the question of whether light is a particle or a wave: both, simultaneously. Light appears as a wave if you ask it "a wave question," and it appears as a particle when you ask it "a particle question." This reminds us that our observations will always be the observations of observers. Science will always be a human science, a *saving of the appearances*. There is no such thing as a "pure science," because our hypotheses hinge on what questions we ask our donkeys. Balaam the scientist and Balaam the poet might live very different stories, but in the end, any scientist who chillingly determines to be "objective" will never really know the deep wholeness of a woman or a tree or a donkey. Only affection and intimacy reveal to us the deeper qualities of creation. We see through a veil dimly, and as we shall explore later, how we know is shaped by how we love.[19]

God walked *in* the garden, but we are *of* the garden. The space between the species and the specimen is not so great. In Atomland we are isolated from our surroundings; we "objectively observe" an "environment" in search of "facts." But in Christendom we are invited to lovingly *participate* in creation, and thus our fingers are always dirty. Unlike God, we are not able to step outside. Our five fallible senses, our invented instruments, our language, invite us to participate in creation *as creatures*. There is a ceiling to human knowledge, and only divine revelation can install skylights.

Most of us do not read philosophy books on materialism. So how did we become materialists? The model created by academics filters down to the courtrooms, to the classrooms, and, finally, to popular culture, where it is absorbed by teens and children and ordinary adults who will never read a philosophy book. It becomes prejudiced and thoughtless habit. We might think we live in a world of pristine MacBooks and J.Crew sweaters, a world so advanced it need not bother with threadbare poetry and tattered religion. But this ideology is born out of a religion—even if it's the religion of New York elitism, newscaster exaggeration, newspeak, Microsoft, McDonald's, and MTV. Behind every science research journal, calendar, business model, children's book, or pop song is a constellation of assumptions about the kind of creatures we are. Even if these ideologies claim not to be religious, they weave our religious narrative, for human beings are inherently religious.

Chapter 8

No One Is Listening

The golden calf of Atomland is found in the forging of *consilience*, which is scientism's supposed "unity of all knowledge." The coherence of creation in Christendom is not anything like consilience, however; its poetry is nothing like what some scientists call "the presence of poetry."[1] For those who believe in the crucified, resurrected Christ, the unity of all knowledge is found in Christ, but under the spell of scientism, unity is found in the laws of physics.[2]

In fact, in Atomland the *unknown* is now shorthand for the *to-be-known*. Science, they say, will eventually answer everything. If it does not know something, it does not know it *yet*. Within this rubric, the pursuit of knowledge leads us to kill to dissect, probing for the answer with little room for respect, wonder, or reverence.[3] But the building of the Tower of Babel did not culminate in consilience, rather in confusion. What if some things are simply not knowable, and to pretend otherwise is to play God, to eat from the Tree of Knowledge of Good and Evil? How will we dispose of enormous amounts of nuclear waste? *We don't know yet.* Where does the physical universe come from? *We don't know yet.* Why is there human suffering? *We don't know yet.*[4] In the face of human suffering, Scientism's ideology, dogmatism, and desperate optimism are well-nigh bankrupt.

What if the idolatry of Atomland is guilty of something ultimately immoral and malevolent? "[Philosophers] will draw this indictment," Wilson writes, "*conflation, simplism, ontological reductionism, scientism*, and other sins made official by the hissing suffix. To which I plead guilty, guilty, guilty."[5] Indeed. Reductionism, blind optimism, and the machine are at the heart of modern ideology, an ideology that comes to fruition not only in animal testing, drug abuse, pesticides, agribusiness, and the horrors of twentieth-century psych wards, but also Mauthausen, Dresden, Hiroshima, and Da Nang. And in projects like Gunther von Hagens's Body Worlds, in which he plasticizes and displays the human body for the public, as if objectification and exploitation are justified in the name of education and entertainment, as if humans were not fearfully and wonderfully wrought and bearing the very breath and likeness of God. Until only a few years ago, Christians in all times and in all places cared passionately about the human body, especially when it had "fallen asleep" (our word *cadaver* comes from the Latin word *cadere*, "to fall"). In Christendom, a cadaver is not a meaningless blob of atoms. It is a sleeping *creature*, a gift from God unable to be desacralized, denigrated, or commodified.

It is truly strange that we think we are so advanced *because of* science and technology. The Nuremberg Code of medical ethics was not founded on a new biochemical discovery, but on an old and poetic conviction. Dr. Eduard Wirths at the Auschwitz concentration camp was a very different kind of doctor than Hildegard of Bingen at the monastery in Rupertsberg, and the difference is not that Wirths was more advanced or evolved. Science is but a tool in the hands of villains and saints; but can science discern which is which? On its own, biology can no more argue against abortion and euthanasia as it can defend human dignity and love. It must build its case for the *value* of human life from some other discipline.

Scientism is not just a methodology; it is a worldview, a "plausibility structure," to use sociologist Peter Berger's phrase. Nothing is wrong with scientific inquiry or technology, but we should not assume that this quest can be done outside the lordship of Christ, the Logos (λογος, *logos*), the Creator and Sustainer of all matter. "Since every science ... is concerned with the Trinity before all else," wrote Bonaventure, "every science must necessarily present some trace of this same Trinity."[6] Our fault has been to compartmentalize the incarnation and resurrection of Jesus, to segregate God's activity on earth from our scientific inquiry of the very same earth. Hark! The herald angels sing, but the shepherds are splitting atoms and the wise men are in business school, and no one is listening.

Chapter 9

Breakfast at the Modern

So I brought my friend Britta to the Modern Café, the bar where I had the crazy-ass epiphany that miracles are possible because Christ is the key to creation. This particular Minneapolis locale has a classic, cozy vibe. A huge swordfish hangs on the wall, and the cherry-stained furniture sharply contrasts with the sea-foam green tiles and upholstery. The barkeeps remember your name (and your poison) after you've visited just a few times. Most important, the Modern's hearty bacon and eggs strata is much savorier than the usual grab-and-go fare at lesser dens. We ordered a couple holy trinities of breakfasts and sat warming our hands on mugs of coffee. It was snowing outside. The bar was packed.

I took a large gulp of coffee and leaned back in my barstool. "I need you to check me on something," I said, looking up at the swordfish.

"Go on," Britta said.

"I don't know where I'm going with this. Maybe nowhere." I was silent for a minute, trying to gather my thoughts. I really wanted to hear what Britta thought of it all, because she is very wise. She's in school studying Italian, French, Spanish, and a little Portuguese. She travels Europe with a camera and journal, drinking wine, learning the languages of different countries, and somehow earning a degree at the same time. She also happens to be wonderfully in love with Jesus and can't seem to get enough of him. She is one of those girls who carries her Bible with her everywhere and is always reading it. She can't stop talking about Jesus and the Bible. That is why I call her when I'm thinking too much.

And so I began to explain to her how I had been wondering if popular Christianity implicitly, and sometimes even explicitly, works from the presuppositions of scientism, of "Atomland." We often have 'God of the gaps' theories, as if knowledge begins with our experiments and not with God's revelation. I told her about my crazy-ass theory and how I'm praying for a holy renaissance.

Britta patiently listened as we waited for our plates.

"Well, I don't know," Britta mused, grabbing a few packets of sugar. "When Christians are born again, they might not wake up speaking Spanish and dancing like Buzz Lightyear. At least not Christians I know. Most of them don't even dance. But they *do* wake up to see the whole world differently, especially our ideas of love and time and people."

"You're right, of course," I said. "But I still wonder if the Christian culture as a whole today has accepted the idea that God lives in the margins where scientific knowledge tapers out. It's like we're recovering secularists in denial. We just add a rosy hue to our secret secularism."

"You're gonna need to unpack that a little more."

The barkeep topped off our mugs, and I gathered my thoughts.

"Okay. Track me here, and see if I'm making any sense," I began. "If Christ is not our starting point, something *other* than Christ is.

The American Dream, for example. I think when we forget that Jesus has practical applications for every corner of human life, we (often unconsciously) stuff Jesus into a box and get on with 'real life,' by which we mean our cars, Walmart, the new business merger, and so on. We start to manage churches like businesses instead of churches. Our worship services imitate the liturgy of the megamall or the Super Bowl halftime show—not because we're trying to reach the culture, but because we actually *are* the culture. Am I making any sense?"

"Keep going," she said.

"I just wonder if some Christians think our churches should be designed like malls because they actually think Jesus is a product that can be marketed, purchased, and consumed. I wonder if some Christians manage our churches like businesses not because the modern business management model can be helpful but because they believe it is a better paradigm for church than the ecclesial model of the apostles and the historic church catholic."

"So you're wondering if we're secularists in Christian costumes?" Britta asked.

"Exactly," I said.

"We lack holy vision," she pressed on. "No imagination. No spiritual transformation. No—"

"No earthly idea of heaven!"

Britta thought for a minute, slowly stirring her coffee with her legs crossed and looking very cosmopolitan. "Well, if worldviews were *le café*," she mused, looking into her mug. "I would say a lot of us Christians have definitely settled for the cheap stuff. At least the mechanical flavor of our coffee is covered over with sugar and cream. At least our secular worldview is sweetened with a Christian supplement. We just dare to call the Sweet'N Low 'God.'"

Just then the barkeep brought us our plates.

"Sweet'N Low is *my* God!" he boomed theatrically, giving Britta a wink. Britta rolled her eyes, and we dug in.

"I think that's a great way to put it," I continued, unfolding a napkin. "Think about it. How many sermons have you heard about 'getting' saved, as if you were purchasing Soul Insurance?"

"More than a few," she said.

"Have you ever noticed they usually start with the quiet assumption that everything from the hills of Tuscany to Orion's belt exists on its own, without Christ? Were it not for sin, everything in the material world would be just fine. But because of sin, Jesus comes flying in, like an alien from outer space, to save us from sin and from 'mere matter.' The gospel is presented as if there is a separation between heaven and earth, and Jesus is the bridge."

"We assume that there is a separation between the natural and the supernatural," she clarified, "like you were saying earlier."

I nodded.

"But now that I think about it, when I read the Bible, I am reminded that they are *never* separated. Jesus is not only my Savior but also my Creator. From the very beginning in Genesis, he is involved and active in the world. It's like," she paused, looking for the right word and playing with the salt and pepper shakers, "it's like the holy is lurking in every corner, like anything could be a revelation of God's presence."

Britta pulled out her Bible as if it were sacred. Its cheap cardboard binding was in shreds. A map of the Paris Metro was poking out somewhere between Job and the Psalms. She opened to Colossians and read aloud: "For by him all things were created: things in heaven and on earth, visible and invisible, whether thrones or powers or rulers or authorities; all things were created by him and for him. He is before all things, and in him all things hold together" (1:16 – 17).

I blinked.

"I've never really thought about it too much, but for Christians everything carries an extra dimension," she concluded, beaming. "Everything is Christ-shaped. Jesus is not an afterthought. He is more than chicken noodle soup for the soul. He is the architect and lover of everything that exists. You know, Ty, the more I read the Bible, the more the whole world starts to look like a mini-Bible, a chapter in God's big story." She looked me straight in the eyes. "Well, what do you want?"

"I want Christians to truly know the love of Christ and to allow that love to completely transform their outlook on all of reality. I want the gospel to be incarnated in their daily lives."

"I want that with you."

"Will you pray for a holy renaissance with me?"

"I will."

And we prayed right there at the bar, prayed that we would not compartmentalize our faith or turn it into something abstract, that God would not give up on us for whom it is difficult to believe. Plain and simple. Direct and specific.

I think Britta was right about the "extra dimension." When we fail to acknowledge it, we miss out on the truth of who Christ is and how we can be swept up into him — the story of *entheosis*, the divinization and the in-Godding of humanity. We forget that we can join in the great salvation story of the crucified, resurrected Christ. He is the Center and the Circumference, the Beginning and the End, our All in All.[1] Is that something you should put on a bumper sticker and slap on the back of your minivan? Of course not — that would be trashy. But it is something you should stamp on your heart, indelibly. "Think straight," says Paul. "Awaken to the holiness of life. No more playing fast and loose with the resurrection facts. Ignorance of God is a luxury you can't afford in times like these" (1 Cor. 15:34 MSG).

Too often we Christians believe in Jesus as if he were a fancy ornament on a building wrought from some other quarry than Christendom. The stone that the builders rejected had not become the cornerstone. But "if all we get out of Christ is a little inspiration for a few short years, we're a pretty sorry lot" (1 Cor. 15:19 MSG). We are called to believe Jesus is God of the universe, not just a nice moral teacher. And we are called to become holy fools for Christ.

It doesn't matter how silly belief in Jesus Christ might look to the people living in Atomland.[2] In a 1912 letter, Albert Einstein wrote: "The more success the quantum theory has, the sillier it looks." Sometimes the better the theory, the sillier it seems. The word *silly*, after all, used to mean "blessed." In the shadow of the cross, any theory can become *theoria*, the process of encountering God, of beholding creation in the light of the Creator — not only through attentive watchfulness in the lab, but through contemplative prayer in the heart. Theories can be paths to *theosis*, final union with Christ. *Theoria* is possible because God is present everywhere, even in the material world, because we live in a world where donkeys have talked and where Jesus once trod. "We may ignore, but we can nowhere evade, the presence of God," wrote C. S. Lewis. "The world is crowded with Him. He walks everywhere *incognito*."[3]

Like my friend Britta, we must look for the Words of God in the text of creation.

> *"For my thoughts are not your thoughts,*
> *neither are your ways my ways,"*

declares the LORD.
"As the heavens are higher than the earth,
      so are my ways higher than your ways
      and my thoughts than your thoughts.
As the rain and the snow
      come down from heaven,
and do not return to it
      without watering the earth
and making it bud and flourish,
      so that it yields seed for the sower and bread for the eater,
so is my word that goes out of my mouth:
      It will not return to me empty,
but will accomplish what I desire
      and achieve the purpose for which I sent it." (Isa. 55:8 – 11)

Part 3

The Coherency of Creation

In Which Stephen the Philistine and Tyler get ready for Christmas, and it is possible to know everything. Reason can be trusted, and people cannot "shop" for truth. Modern science is just as anthropomorphic and poetic as medieval science. The medieval posture is not specialized but is integrated and holistic. Sometimes Christianity is very pagan looking because paganism is confused Christianity. We begin to smuggle from the Egyptians.

The wonderful, inconceivably intricate tapestry is being taken apart strand by strand; each thread is being pulled out, torn up, and analyzed; and at the end even the memory of the design is lost and can no longer be recalled.

—Erwin Chargaff, *Heraclitean Fire*

Serious historians are abandoning the absurd notion that the medieval church persecuted all scientists as wizards. It is very nearly the opposite of the truth.

—G. K. Chesterton, *Saint Thomas Aquinas*

Chapter 10

Can Reason Be Trusted?

G. K. Chesterton once said that it is impossible to enjoy anything without humility—but that today we are humble in the wrong way. "A man was meant to be doubtful of himself, but undoubting about the truth; this has been exactly reversed. Nowadays the part of a man that a man does assert is exactly the part he ought not to assert—himself. The part he doubts is exactly the part he ought not to doubt—the Divine Reason."[1] My generation of young adults tends to think that truth comes and goes willy-nilly, and so we believe in ourselves. We don't know what's true or even know how to find out what's true. We don't really know what's truly valuable. We just have our own personal experience of what we think is valuable. We don't feel like anything is truly trustworthy beyond ourselves, which means we are left with nothing but ourselves. That's why we think it's so important to succeed or not to have any regrets or to be always moving in "a positive direction." This plays out in our daily lives in the strangest ways.[2]

For example, today we young adults imagine that sometime in the future we will outgrow Phase 1 of adulthood—a phase peppered with travel, parties, hookups, and money making—and finally settle down into Phase 2, where we'll get married, have children, enter a serious career, buy a house or condo, and begin a middle-class mass-consumer lifestyle with all the appropriate accoutrements of dogs and friends and cars and televisions. There is almost no conversation about care for children or the elderly or a general husbandry of our communities, and there is certainly no conversation about serving God or discovering and serving the truth. We do not think in terms of maturity or responsibility or duty, but in terms of success and self-fulfillment. The idea is that if *I* settle down, *I* will be able to do what *I* want to do with Phase 2.

And so we are obsessed with ourselves, and our individualistic, consumerist attitudes shape our philosophy and outlook toward all of life. There is no fact, higher truth, objective reality, or law that is independent of our subjective personal experience. Our imaginations are clouded over with a deep confusion and uncertainty about what is objectively right and wrong or good and evil. How can there be identifiable and objective truth if we are unable to know anything beyond ourselves? After all, isn't truth just a social construction, what we picked up from our parents? What if other kids in other cultures might believe in some other truth? The idea is that whatever is true is true for people because people make it true by believing it. But I imagine G. K. Chesterton would respond, what is true is true because it is objectively true, regardless of whether we believe it to be true. When it comes to belief, my generation is what we always have been: shoppers. But we are so indecisive and fickle that we never really own anything—no higher good, no religion, not even ourselves. If there is no God, all morality is subjective and arbitrary and internal.

I'm not out to prove the existence of God, but I am out to be reasonable and consistent. I don't want to pretend we live in a world that is meaningless and chaotic when every day we live as though it is meaningful and ordered. Bertrand Russell famously claimed that a person is "the product of causes.... His origin, his growth, his hopes and fears, his loves and his beliefs, are but the outcome of accidental collocations of atoms."[3] In other words, human beings are something like serendipitous catastrophes, collisions, casualties. Beethoven's symphonies and Shakespeare's plays, every loving embrace and every martyr's death are nothing more than happy atomic crashes, fender benders in a fender-bender universe. Though there is not an atom of proof that God made the universe, there's also no way to prove that God did not make the universe. Yet everywhere we look, we find suggestions, hints as to which is more likely.

For example, it's no small thing that we live in a world, not a chaos. The more we learn, the more we see that our universe is not chaotic but is ordered, patterned and designed, meaningful and with purpose. This is why we are comfortable building bridges and ice fishing. If the world were not a world but a chaos, we would not dare to cross a bridge, for engineers could not trust physics, or stand on a frozen lake, for it could instantly melt at 14° Fahrenheit. All scientific, inductive reasoning suggests that tomorrow ice will melt at temperatures higher than 32° under the standard conditions of today. Inductive reasoning cannot *prove* this regularity of nature will continue; it can only take it in good *faith* because it's reasonable. If "reason" is merely the accidental banging of atoms and twitching synapses, it certainly cannot be trusted. For us to take any stock in reason, even to take any stock in the inductive reasoning of the science lab, reason itself must be over and above nature. It must come from some other source than a mysterious bang, however big.

Like arguments for God, the construal that ethics, love, good, and evil are all an adaptation for the survival of the species can neither be proved nor disproved. Unlike the arguments for God, however, this construal is not founded on reason: why would we trust reason or truth if it is nothing but the slipshod modifications of electrons and neurons?

We think because God thinks. We know because God knows. We speak because God speaks. We use words to describe reality because God used words to create reality. We do not simply choose in an arbitrary fashion to attach labels to collections of meaningless objects. Though it is true that people name donkeys "donkeys" and nitrogen "nitrogen," it does not necessarily follow that in naming what we discover we create meaning out of what would otherwise be a meaningless vacuum. Though it is true that people read meaning into the text of creation, it is also true that the text of creation is already rich with the Author's intention. Meaning is already there. Though Atomland's ideology might cloak it from sight, the world is full of hints, echoes, and rumors of God. It resounds with a rationality and morality and meaning that we did not invent but received. It is by the grace of God that we can reason and love and truly know anything. "By your light we see light" (Ps. 36:9, my paraphrase).

Chapter 11

Smuggling from the Egyptians

All truth is God's truth. But you do not have to be a Christian to catch glimpses of it, sometimes even to behold vivid and precise visions. For example, one does not have to be a Christian to be a good doctor; and, generally speaking, I would rather see a good doctor than a not-so-good Christian doctor. Though Christ made the human body, one need not know Christ to know the human body. Similarly, the world is resonant with God's truth and goodness, and you do not need to know Christ to perceive this truth and goodness. In a Logos-created and Logos-infused world, people cannot help but stumble upon the truth. This is why despite the faulty premises of scientism, Christians do not need to throw away their laptops or refuse modern medicine. The discoveries of astrophysics are beautiful discoveries. The data acquired about how the brain works is very helpful data. The City of God has always borrowed knowledge from the City of Man—even science, even paganism—and brought it into the larger context of God's salvation stories.

In the past, people used the phrase "despoiling the Egyptians" (cf.

Ex. 12:36) for instances when Christians recognized that although things like Greek rhetoric or the Roman arch and dome were pagan ideas, there was truth in them. For example, the Greek philosopher Pythagoras (580–500 BC) sought to interpret the entire physical cosmos in terms of numbers through systematic and mystical study. Even though Christians interpret the entire physical cosmos in terms of Christ, they have found great truth and usefulness in Pythagoras's theorem of the right-angled triangle. Because all truth is God's truth, geometry is no longer only pagan but also Christian.

By *pagan* we often mean "anyone who is not a Christian," similar to how ancient Jews called anyone who was not a Jew a *Gentile*. Sometimes *paganism* also calls to mind the dark arts, witchcraft, or Satan worship. But in this book, when we think of paganism, we should not think of black magic or sorcery; rather, we should think of walking through the Louvre in Paris or visiting the Pantheon in Rome, of reading Homer or Virgil or studying Renaissance humanism. Here *paganism* means neither simply anything-not-Christian nor the dark arts but rather those myths and cultural influences on Christianity that are artful and illustrative of the truth even though they are extrabiblical.

"What has Athens to do with Jerusalem," asked Tertullian, "or the Academy with the church?"[1] What does Atomland have to do with Christendom? How can we use science without ourselves joining the pop cult of scientism? How can we adopt what is good and useful in the surrounding culture without selling out?

The stonemasons of Christendom have always added the good and beautiful bricks of culture to the cathedral of the church. The medievals, in particular, were masters of despoiling the Egyptians. Just look at a Gothic cathedral. The builders took the principles of pagan architecture and used them to point to Christ, especially by emphasizing verticality and light. In the ogival arch, they directed the old Roman arch upward, pointing it like an arrow to Christ. In their creation of the ribbed vault, the old dome was directed toward God. Everything from clusters of columns, vaults, flying buttresses, and the cruciform pattern of the building as a whole was intended to remind people of the kingdom of God. Cathedrals were the skyscrapers of the day, and while today's skyscrapers remind us of the power of money, the cathedrals' steeples and spires, towering above the buildings of the town, pointed people's gaze heavenward. Like the apostle Paul on Mars Hill, medieval architects took the best of pagan architecture and baptized it into the Christian narrative. They could do this because the reality of Jesus and his kingdom was their fixed starting point, their North Star, the one thing they did not question.

When Christians live in the light of Christ, they are always smuggling from the Egyptians. They can't help it, because everything has the potential to testify to our Savior's glory. "God made Man so that he was capable of coming in contact with reality," said G. K. Chesterton; "and those whom God hath joined, let no man put asunder."[2] In Christendom, knowledge cannot be compartmentalized or reduced to the world of specialists. It is one multifaceted diamond. Jesus is the unity of the universe. There is, therefore, a unity to knowledge that transcends both consilience's reductionism and modernism's compartmentalization. In many ways, I think we have forgotten how to smuggle from the Egyptians, how to take what is good in other disciplines outside theology and to integrate them and lift them up in theology, "the queen of sciences."[3]

Because the medieval Christians of yore were masters of celebrating the coherency of creation in Christ, it was not long before I steered my donkey down the overgrown and nearly forgotten medieval pathways. And so these next few chapters explore that sweet and loamy swath, the *medium aevum*, the Middle Age. On a low and humble ass, we'll explore how the Christians there plundered Egypt, how they took the popular myths and sciences of their day and baptized them into the kingdom of God.

By the time I was seriously considering this idea, Minneapolis was covered in two feet of snow, and on an arctic December morning, Stephen the Philistine and I went shopping for his Christmas tree.

"I want it to be big and green," he said enthusiastically, giving considerable volume to the words *big* and *green*. He was wearing an enormous Santa cap that cascaded down his back.

After a good half hour of laboring to find the best tree, I coyly sidled up next to Stephen to see how he was fairing and to ask him a question. He was gawking at the fattest, tallest Christmas tree for sale.

"Is it possible to know everything?" I asked.

Stephen slowly looked away from the mighty tree and down at me. Over the years, Stephen has gained a reputation for being the go-to man for tackling the most difficult intellectual questions. His stern brow and know-it-all smirk make him anything but affable. He turned his fierce gaze upon me.

"Haven't you heard of Thomas Young?" he asked, his large mustache collecting ice. I had not. "He's this British guy who had such a lust for learning that he studied four hundred languages, conducted experiments that laid the foundation for quantum physics, decoded the Rosetta Stone, and just when he was about to die, invented life insurance. He knew everything."

"Whoa! Really?"

"Really."

Our breath hung in the frosty air.

"The only problem is that human knowledge has exploded since

1829, when he died. No single brain could ever possibly know it all anymore — not even his. Do you think Sir Thomas could mix the perfect Mojito? Land an airplane? Break dance? Repair a Volkswagen motor? Make a pair of Nikes? Spot a pair of fake Prada sunglasses?" He gave me a grave look. "I doubt it."

I nodded.

"They didn't even have Wikipedia back then," I joshed.

"Yeah, and they didn't have birth control either," Stephen said, sensing my sarcasm.

"I just wish our lives weren't so compartmentalized and narrow," I said.

"Tyler, I know you're really into medieval monks and polymaths and all that, but it's not such a bad thing that the world is now ruled by specialists. Wikipedia might be the world's finest hour, when we've gathered the knowledge in an easy to click through, absolutely comprehensive guide to everything, ever."

He walked up and shook a large tree, and dead needles fell all over the place. He snorted, and we turned to find a tree whose dead needles hadn't been spray-painted green.

"Want to know how to build a nuclear bomb? Want to learn how to fix a fridge? Want to construct your own computer, like Oliver?" With this he smiled, and his mustache took a little bow. "Read from the experts, the specialists, my friend. Sir Thomas would be proud."

I grimaced. I don't think the world needs more experts.

Today we are encouraged to become expensively trained to do one thing, and one thing only. Once I come home from, say, design adhesives, I sit down to a dinner I know only through the plastic box I bought it in. I know, vaguely, that my food contains poisons, like how I vaguely know my job in adhesives creates poisons. I spend the evening with my children watching other experts on television. My kids have spent their day in the care of education experts, soccer and health experts, or perhaps daycare experts. I have no clue what I'd do if I lost my job or if the utility companies went under or if the garbage collectors went on strike or if agribusiness collapsed or if my wireless Internet connection were disabled.

There is very little I can take pride in that I have produced myself, that I *know*. My wife is an expert in, say, prosthodontics (artificial teeth). I do not understand what she does. I do not understand most things, even my body. I do not have the capacity to understand. So I consult certified experts who specialize in impotency and anxiety, and they prescribe me a pill designed by pharmaceutical specialists. And then, perhaps, I am fortunate to discover the Kentucky Aristotelian Wendell Berry and to read on some auspicious day, "The specialist system fails from a personal point of view because a person who can do only one thing can do virtually nothing for himself. In living in the world by his own will and skill, the stupidest peasant or tribesman is more competent than the most intelligent worker or technician or intellectual in a society of specialists."[4]

My mind snapped back to reality as Stephen began to goggle another conifer.

"The problem with a world of specialists," I started up again, "is that specialists know a lot about very little. They think they under-stand the big picture, but they don't. They've spent a lot of time study-ing one little thing, but they have never studied how that one thing fits into everything else. This is how you get biology teachers who think biology has somehow replaced theology or philosophers who think physics is irrelevant. But everything is connected."

Stephen gave a humph and, with much resolve, hoisted his tree of choice.

"This one should do," he proclaimed.

I shook it. "You're right."

"Of course I'm right," he said, as if he were rarely otherwise.

We proudly shouldered the tree to the Boy Scout to pay. It appeared that another customer was shopping from her heated SUV, making the poor boy drag evergreens to her door so she could appraise them. Lipstick covered her Starbucks coffee cup, which she used to gesticulate her yeas and nays.

Stephen shook his head. He took off his mittens and started counting up the cash.

We carried the tree home, lashed about the top of my little red truck, and then lugged it into Stephen's apartment, immediately wishing we had a vacuum-brandishing concierge behind us. Needle droppings were everywhere. Then there was the problem of getting it to stand up straight. I slid underneath the conifer and tightened the stand around the trunk, pine needles falling into my mouth and ears and betwixt my collar and my neck, while Stephen shouted decrees.

"Move it right. Yes, that's right. Now toward me. Left. Very good. No! Too far," he bellowed. "Move it back. More. No. Much too far, you medieval pedant!"

Forsooth, I did feel a little medieval, rotating the tree as directed. I was using my body and geometry and my imagination to celebrate the holiday of Christ's incarnation through the pagan practice of right-ing the evergreen. I felt rather accomplished sitting back on Stephen's couch, the tree finally erect, a hot tea in hand, the cold world at last far away. And while Stephen busied himself with twinkle lights, I pulled from my saddlebag the books I had purchased for my holy pilgrimage to read about the medieval mind.

Chapter 12

How to Know Everything

When we peer into the recesses of the Middle Age, we discover the polymath, the person of wide-ranging knowledge and learning. Specialization is blind to the inherent continuity and harmony of all things. In the world of specialization, a person gets so focused on one thing, he or she forgets about everything else. Although the medievals did not know *as much* as we know today, the *way* they knew was broader and more holistic.

If it could be learned, the people of the Middle Age learned it. This is because central to ancient Christianity's intellectual life are the seven liberal arts, the syllabus or curriculum that shaped all that could be known. They were called *liberal* (*liber*, free) because they were the proper courses of study for a student to become free and more fully human. A common misunderstanding is that the Enlightenment gave us our love of reason and the seven disciplines.[1] But the liberal arts were born of the Middle Age. At that time schoolmen were mining old words and cutting them into a current coin. At every turn they were codifying and classifying and creating the conceptual foundation we now build upon. "Nobody who understands the amount of pain and energy which go to the creation of new instruments of thought can feel anything but respect for the philosophy of the Middle Ages."[2]

In late antiquity, a man named Martianus Capella took it upon himself to divide knowledge into seven easily referenced categories, which are themselves broken up into two sets, the trivium (grammar, rhetoric, logic), and the quadrivium (arithmetic, astronomy, music, geometry). Medicine and law were deemed earthly, not divine, and remained separate from the liberal arts. They do to this day. With the fall of Rome and in the face of political and social upheaval, an Italian scholar named Cassiodorus introduced the seven disciplines to the monastic life, and monasteries thus became scriptoria, centers for the preservation and dissemination of classical (that is, Roman and Greek) texts. This laid the foundation for the university system we know today, but also textbooks. The *artes liberales* sought to broaden persons' general knowledge, to develop rational and imaginative thought, and to equip them to rightly handle the tools of reason, experience, and the authorities (the books). If a man was in a heated debate, he could appeal to three credible sources. He would, for example, establish a geometric truth by reason, establish a historical truth by authority (by the old books, *auctores*), and determine that the milk had gone bad from firsthand experience.

Do you know how very few of us could actually build a nuclear bomb or a space rocket or an iPod, or even make an ibuprofen tablet? Yet what the learned have discovered influences our popular understanding of the universe and how we relate to it. Well, that's what it was like in the Middle Age. Although study in the seven liberal arts was usually available only to the rich who could afford it, it still influenced the lives of the peasantry. Even though they didn't know everything, they lived in a world where what could be known was ordered and meaningful. And medieval men with the leisure and money to afford such an education were indeed invited to know everything that they knew could be known. In this sense, it was actually possible to know everything.

The medieval scholastics and poets were clerkly, bookish, and obsessed with manuscripts from time-tested *auctores*, "thise olde wise."[3] Their tidy-mindedness lent them a disposition to sorting, synthesizing, and sprucing up.[4] Science and religion were not polar opposites but different ways of describing and questioning the same thing. You know how in *Romeo and Juliet* Friar Lawrence rambles on about earth and nature, plants, herbs, stones, and their true qualities, virtues, and vices? It's because friars and monks and scholars were not experts in just one field. They were doctors, astrologers, farmers, bakers, alchemists, theologians, and poets all at once. The more these schoolmen learned, the more enchanted they became.

Chapter 13

A World of Desires, Not Laws

*E*xploring ancient and enchanted Christianity, we quickly discover that those early believers plundered knowledge from all corners of the world and integrated it into a single, Christ-shaped model of the world. Unlike in Atomland, there are no cubicles in Christendom. Back then one could not compartmentalize knowledge into little cubbies, as if things were not connected in Christ. There was no segregation, no bigotry, no shoving certain disciplines to the back of the bus. All of life—from how to raise a family to how to practice medicine—was interwoven and joined together.

This coherency of creation, this unity of all life and knowledge in Jesus, changed the basic presuppositions about how the whole world works. They used different metaphors than Atomland, because in Christendom the world was not meaningless and machinelike but meaningful and Godlike.

Unlike the pagan philosophers, however, who deify the universe rather than seek the Creator of the universe,[1] medieval Christians believed with the apostolic fathers in the doctrine of creation *ex nihilo*, that "nothing is coeternal with God."[2] They were not pantheists. In the biblical view of creation, they believed, God and the world are not synonymous. Rather, God the Creator arranges and finishes all of creation by his own power, and he sustains all things, visible and invisible, with his will.[3] Yet though the world is not God himself, they did not drain it of spiritual significance and divine presence. The supernatural order of cosmos accepted the oneness of God and the goodness of creation.

These early believers perceived human life to be a part of a grand drama that gave context and meaning to suffering and joy. Their poems and ballads recalled tales from the distant past, a common heritage. They were part of a story being told; their lives were a small chapter of that story. The stage of this grand drama was Planet Earth, a world with its own curtains and lights and backstage hands. Earth was governed by Fortune, who had influence over the lives of men. Earth was also full of fairies — not fairies like Tinker Bell, but *longaevi*, "longlivers," who "haunt the woods, glades, and groves, and lakes and springs and brooks; whose names are Pans, Fauns ... Satyrs, Silvans, Nymphs."[4] While some fairies were evil and dangerous, others were merry and elusive. Others were prophets, and still others were erotic and seductive. All of them could relate to humanity's fears and failures, sorrows and successes.

The result of this fairy-filled Europe was a world packed with community to the corners. One had to be careful where one mopped and swept. Angels and demons were bald fact. The low-slung sky was jam-packed with the invisible company of heaven, the nine orders of angels — not cuddly ceramic-looking children, but terrifying spirits. To Chaucer, a cherub was a creature of fire. Dante's angels are virile, of cosmic nobility. Back then the nativity story could be told without the listeners even blinking. They would have sung Charles Wesley's "Hark! The Herald Angels Sing," believing they were joining the triumph of the skies. When nineteenth-century Christian Phillips Brooks wrote "O Little Town of Bethlehem," he wrote with a strong medieval flavor:

> *For Christ is born of Mary, and gathered all above,*
> *While mortals sleep, the angels keep their watch of wondering love.*
> *O morning stars, together proclaim the holy birth!*
> *And praises sing to God the King, and peace to men on earth.*

Looking beyond angels and fairies, the world as a whole was divided into four grades of reality, like the rungs of a ladder: mere existence (e.g., rocks), growing existence (e.g., trees), growing existence with feelings (e.g., dogs), and all of the above with reason (humans).

All of creation possessed *anima*, or "soul," and there were three grades of *anima*: the *vegetable soul*, common to all plants; the *sensitive soul*, which adds to the vegetable soul life and feeling, and the *rational soul*, which is how we think. You and I have all three. The four grades of reality and the three souls in living things radiated qualities. Thus, a donkey's bray actually radiated donkey-ness.

Today when we say a donkey's bray is amusing, we mean that the amusement takes place within ourselves. But to medievals, the donkey's bray actually radiated amusement. When a herb was said to possess a *virtue*, or when an eye was said to be *evil*, the bones of a saint to be *holy*, or a red sunrise to be *benign* or *malign*, the medieval mind believed these objects emanated these activities of the soul, which they understood in terms of sympathies and antipathies. And so it was said that rocks fell because of their sympathies, because they *desired* to fall. And it was said that rocks did not fall up because of their antipathies, their *dislike* for going up.

The world and the inhabitants thereof possessed a living spirit. There was a homing instinct in everything that compelled it to do what it was made to do.[5] In the novel *Anne of Green Gables*, which takes place around the turn of the nineteenth to twentieth century, we see a truly medieval perspective when Anne says, "I've made up my mind to enjoy this drive.... Oh, look, there's one little early wild rose out! Isn't it lovely? Don't you think it must be glad to be a rose? Wouldn't it be nice if roses could talk? I'm sure they could tell us such lovely things."[6]

Few share Anne's medieval imagination. In Atomland they would say Anne *personified* (a relatively new eighteenth-century word) the rose. Her idea of how the world works is *anthropomorphic* (an even newer nineteenth-century word). But we could just as easily ask the modern scientist, "Do you really think that nature works in terms of 'obedience' to 'laws'?"[7] Was Newton's apple aware of an ordinance issued by a lawmaker that apples must fall? Is there really an eleventh commandment for rocks that says, "Thou shalt not fall upwards"? Of course not. Neither were medieval people referring to some law or commandment when they talked about how a stone's "purpose" is to fall, how it "strives" to fall. Talking about rocks having a "homing instinct" is not any more "anthropomorphic" than talking about rocks "obeying laws" like citizens of a city-state. Neither metaphor should be read literally.[8] Should we cast the universe in the image of our legal system, or should we wrap it in the likeness of our desires and hopes?[9] Although sometimes helpful, the word *anthropomorphic* too often assumes there is no real connection or correlation between humans and the world. But what if the distance between *creaturae* and *creation* is not so great?

Today technology is the most popular metaphor for describing how our bodies work. If weather and the seasons, planting and harvest, night and day, shape our daily life, elements like air and fire and water serve to explain the mystery of the human body. But if machines are run by gears and pulleys, we tend to think of ourselves in terms of gears and pulleys. If our gadgets are electronic, chemical, or digital, we tend to think of our brains in terms of computing and chemistry. Today we are confident that computers are the way our bodies work, but tomorrow we will chuckle at our naïveté. The "scientific" worldview of today will become the discarded image of tomorrow—not necessarily because we will know more or be "more advanced," but because we simply will have modified our metaphors. So said Dorothy Sayers: "Modern science has not superseded mediaeval thought about the nature of creation, but only the physical picture which accompanied and illustrated it."[10]

It matters which metaphor we use, because metaphors are how we "save the appearances." They are props, arrangements, temporary models. Our vision of the cosmos has implications for what it means to be human and for our understanding of who God is. Though we may plunder everything from Athens to Egypt to NASA, we should never sell out. Christ remains our point of reference, our God, the Lord of all things, not just some things. "Is not the *feel* of a thing as real, as much a fact, as the thing felt?" asked Cecil Day-Lewis. "Is not the conveying of the *quality* or *value* of an experience, therefore, a contribution to knowledge no less useful than the analysis of that experience in terms of physical fact and natural law?"[11]

Anne of Green Gables puts it this way: "I read in a book once that a rose by any other name would smell as sweet, but I've never been able to believe it. I don't believe a rose *would* be as nice if it was called a thistle or a skunk cabbage."[12] The metaphors we use to describe our scientific discoveries shape our imaginations, our posture toward the world, our self-understanding, perhaps even our happiness. How we perceive the whole universe shapes faith, hope, and love.

In part 1 we discovered Balaam and his talking donkey. I shared with you a little part of my story, about how I came to hunger for a God who is not an afterthought, and about how I came to long for a Christianity that is ancient and enchanted. Like knights-errant, we are wandering in search of adventures in a God-bathed world. But the strange assumptions of scientism would have blocked our every turn. And so in part 2, we did battle with the highwaymen and naysayers of Atomland, and in part 3 we reclaimed the unity of the uni-versity and the uni-verse. Starting from different presuppositions, Christendom uses a different paradigm than Atomland to understand how the world works.

God is not a stopgap for the incompleteness of our knowledge. "We are to find God in what we know, not in what we don't know," wrote Dietrich Bonhoeffer in response to reading Carl Friedrich von Weizsäcker's *The World-View of Physics*. The revelation of Jesus Christ is the only starting point for how we can know anything, even ourselves: "He is the centre of life, and he certainly didn't 'come' to answer our unsolved problems."[13] The contemporary mythology of a Godless, meaningless universe is antithetical to even the possibility of Christ. But the old, medieval mythology was sympathetic to a world not only rich with angels and demons and fairies, but with God himself, the

Creator and Sustainer of the universe. This will come into clearer focus later when we uncover the essence of the Lord's Supper, covenant, and what being a "member" of a church is all about. But before we can hobnob with those old ideas and truths, we must first better understand a world where talking donkeys would simply make sense. Let's plunge even deeper into the dark medieval forests of an earlier Christendom, riding nothing less than that beast of burden, an ass.

Part 4

In Thrall to the Heavens

In Which Tyler and his friends go camping, and Oliver shows Tyler his Dr. Dre–endorsed headphones. The night sky is like the vaulted ceiling of a cathedral. The seven heavens are introduced. Our donkey rubs elbows with Thor and Santa Claus. It is suggested that no one can *be* a genius. Jesus is the Lord of time. A medieval monk steps out to pray.

If the whole universe has no meaning, we should never have found out that it has no meaning: just as, if there were no light in the universe and therefore no creatures with eyes, we should never know it was dark. *Dark* would be without meaning.

—C. S. Lewis, *Mere Christianity*

Yet hints come to me from the realm unknown;
Airs drift across the twilight border land,
Ordered with life.

—George MacDonald, *Diary of an Old Soul*

Chapter 14

Our Camping Trip

I remember wanting to go camping last summer, long before Minneapolis was covered in a blanket of white snow and the weather was still warm. I had it all planned out: I was going to spend a night in the woods like an old medieval mystic. No technology. No city lights. Just God and the stars. I cajoled my friends into joining me (one does not simply go into the woods alone). Stephen the Philistine was able to take off work, and so was his French roommate. My redheaded friend Oliver had never been to the woods before. And so the four of us went to the grocery store to buy provisions for our night in the woods: raisins, peanuts, three pounds of M&Ms, several sticks of beef jerky, imperishable doughnuts and cakes, graham crackers, instant mashed potatoes, and thus and such. The list was anything but what a real outdoorsman would bring camping. After a great deal of squabbling and worrying, the sort that floods city mice venturing out into the country, we sallied out into the north woods on my uncle's land to look up into the night sky. After a three-hour drive and a ten-minute hike filled with scary wolf stories, rustling gear and banging pots and pans, we finally set up camp in a patch of woods that opened to sky.

It was anything but serene. I kept wondering why I was in such a bad mood. By the time we set up the tent, it was nearly black. Stephen the Philistine furnished an enormous battery lamp he said he purchased just for our trip. Everyone blinked as it flooded our tent with florescent rays. His French roommate was unpacking bags of candy and taking illicit sips of bourbon. Oliver flipped open his laptop, hooked up his smart phone, and tried to get online. I was trying to figure out how to get air into my sleeping pad. We were soon engrossed in our various tasks and efforts to achieve equilibrium.

"Has anyone seen my adventure shoes?" Stephen asked, turning to me with modest alarm. I had no clue where his adventure shoes were. Just then his cell phone rang loudly in the din. It was his French roommate.

"Eah, I sink I em very lost," we could hear him say a bit frantically from the earpiece.

We suddenly remembered that he had left to find the outhouse over an hour ago. I offered to go find him, trying not to imagine him scampering through the dark woods with flailing arms and unhappy wails. As I was about to head out Oliver unveiled from his enormous backpack an iPod and a huge set of Dr. Dre–endorsed headphones. I was flummoxed.

"Headphones?" I barely asked. This was not the scenario I had envisioned. Oliver let me hold them. They weighed nothing. He saw my look of wonder.

"I can't sleep without music," he said blankly. "These are high-definition headphones, Tyler, and they actually reproduce the tiny intricacies lost with most headphones. They cancel out noise. They have powered amplification. They even have a low-profile connector that easily couples with any music player or mobile phone."

"Does it find Frenchmen?" I asked earnestly.

To make matters worse, when I stepped out into the cool evening, I saw that clouds hid the stars from view. I could not see a thing. We had only just begun, and the trip had already failed. It's embarrassing to admit, but I guess I thought we would stare at Orion, Taurus, or the Pleiades as they would rise into view, no iPods, no cell phones, no bright florescent lamps.

"That's Aries," I might say at last.

"It makes me wonder if there is a God," Oliver might even say.

Stephen would nod solemnly.

Of course, none of this would happen with the clouds out and our technology already filling every corner of the woods. But with Stephen's roommate rescued from the darkness, we soon had a cheery fire dancing in the pit. Propped against the logs, legs thrust out, roasting Oscar Mayer wieners on long sticks, we were finally starting to look like a real coterie of woodsmen. We couldn't see any stars, but at least the company was good. So were the wieners.

Many beers and marshmallows later, I tucked into my sleeping bag and tried to fall asleep to the percussive hisses leaking from Oliver's enormous headphones. The Frenchman was snoring as melodiously as a Christmas cantata. Stephen was still outside by the fire, trying to make even more s'mores. Bumping noises and soft cursings and sounds like big trees being dragged across the forest floor came floating to me through the micro-thin tent wall. It smelled good, whatever it was.

I sighed and unzipped myself from the nylon into the cool July evening. Stephen was crouched over the campfire looking dubiously industrious. The clouds had at last dispersed, and I could see the stars stretching overhead.

Oliver also came swishing out of the tent, small hisses still coming from the headphones straddling his neck.

"Whoa," he said, looking up. "I've never seen so many stars."

"Have you ever been out of the city at night?" I asked.

"Not really," he answered wistfully.

We just stood there gawking at the night sky. Silence filled the woods. I longed—beyond my power to convey—to see God. The sky was arrestingly beautiful. To be honest, I tried to hear God's music up there.

But the stars were quiet. Stephen staggered over and looked up briefly, gave a humph through his mustache, and then staggered on back to where he came from. Soon Oliver turned and went back into the tent. I stood there under the billion stars and thought about how awesome it is that God holds them together, like notes on a page of music. It's a music that is always playing; we just can't hear it because it is constant. But it's there. A free and beautiful jazz.

Chapter 15

But Much Less Like a Ball

When Christians sing with the old poet, "The earth is the LORD's, and everything in it" (Ps. 24:1), or "The heavens declare the glory of God; the skies proclaim the work of his hands" (Ps. 19:1), we believe (or at least we should) that creation conveys something of the Creator and his story. We believe (or at least we should) that loving attention to creation is a path to knowledge and even sanctification. "Where can I go from your Spirit? Where can I flee from your presence? If I go up to the heavens, you are there; if I make my bed in the depths, you are there" (Ps. 139:7–8). Heaven is not an abstract idea but a real activity, ever emerging, ever near.

Today we think of heaven as almost floating somewhere in outer space. Most of us fail to recognize the implied intimacy of the kingdom of heaven in Christianity. In the Bible, "the heavens" are not always hiding behind the stars or locked up behind Saint Peter's gates. Sometimes they are the very air you breathe, the atmosphere that surrounds your body. Although του ουρανου (*tou ouranou*) often means simply heaven,[1] it also means simply the sky, the atmosphere, the air around you.[2] The Lord is here, all around us, *Immanuel*. When Jesus speaks of the Kingdom "at hand," it is an enveloping Kingdom among us (Mark 1:15). When Abraham was about to sacrifice Isaac, God called to him *out of heaven*, "Heaven" being the very air surrounding him (Gen. 22:11, 15). When Jacob dreams of a passageway connecting Earth and Heaven, the Lord is standing *beside him*. He wakes up saying of the place, "God lives here! This is God's home" (Gen. 28:12–19). The manifestation of something like God-fire appearing in the air happened so often that the Israelites came to describe the nearness of God as a "consuming fire."[3] Our words *diary* and *journal* come to us from the old words that mean not only "God," but also "the sky" or "the heavens."[4] Time and the sky and God were all connected. Owen Barfield observes, "When our earliest ancestors looked up to the blue vault, they felt that they saw not merely a place, whether Heavenly or earthly, but the bodily vesture, as it were, of a living Being."[5]

One reason we don't think of the heavens this way is because of what Dallas Willard calls timid translations. For example, in his chapter "What Jesus Knew: Our God-Bathed World" in *The Divine Conspiracy*, Willard observes that in Acts 11:5–9 we see the New American Standard Bible translate του ουρανου in three different ways: "the sky" in verse 5, "the air" in verse 6, and "heaven" in verse 9. But the text tells us that Peter saw a sheet descending through *the atmosphere* (του ουρανου, *tou ouranou*) filled with animals like birds of *the atmosphere*, and that Peter heard God's voice from *the atmosphere* telling him to eat.[6] This changes a lot about what it means to pray the Lord's Prayer: "Our Father, who art in the heavens (τους ουρανους, *tois ouranois*)" (Matt. 6:9, my translation). God is not distant. God inhabits and overflows space and time, the very air we breathe.

For the ancient Jews, God was literally taking up his abode on earth, especially in the Temple. Like the tabernacle in the wilderness, the Temple was the place from which God ruled Israel. The Temple was where God established his domain, where heaven and earth overlapped and interlocked. It was a signpost pointing to a deeper reality. One of the reasons Jesus cleaned out the corruption in the Temple was not to make a statement about economics, but to signal that *he* was the new living, breathing temple (Mark 11:15 – 19). He was claiming to be the messianic King, as N. T. Wright argues.[7] Joshua the Christ, God incarnate, the intersection of heaven and earth. God taking up abode on earth in his only Son.

In old Hebrew theology, space is not empty; space is holy. "Certainly mere space travel is not the way to discover the divine richness that fills all creation," reflects Willard. "That discovery comes through personal seeking and spiritual reorientation, as well as God's responsive act of making himself present to those ready to receive. Only then will we cry with the seraphim, 'Holy! Holy! Holy!' as we find 'the whole earth full of his glory.'"[8] Thus sings the old hymn:[9]

> *O worship the King, all glorious above,*
> *O gratefully sing His pow'r and His love;*
> *Our Shield and Defender, the Ancient of Days,*
> *Pavilioned in splendor and girded with praise.*
>
> *O tell of His might, O sing of His grace,*
> *Whose robe is the light, whose canopy space.*
> *His chariots of wrath the deep thunderclouds form,*
> *And dark is His path on the wings of the storm.*
>
> *Thy bountiful care what tongue can recite?*
> *It breathes in the air, it shines in the light;*
> *It streams from the hills, it descends to the plain,*
> *And sweetly distills in the dew and the rain.*

Christians take Paul at his word when he says that Christ descended to the lower, earthly realm so that he might ascend higher than all the heavens, "in order to fill the whole universe" (Eph. 4:9–10). Heaven is not a long way away, somewhere up in the sky. Heaven and earth coincide and dovetail. Heaven is a different kind of space. Heaven is God's space, his personal dimension. Heaven is the place from where the world is governed. This is why when Luke described Jesus as being "taken up" and hidden by "a cloud," he didn't mean that Jesus was launched somewhere into outer space (Acts 1:9). He meant that Jesus was being *enthroned* as the King of the new creation his life and passion inaugurated (Phil. 2:9–11). If he had not "ascended," he would be in only one place. Having "ascended" into heaven, Jesus is present everywhere. When Jesus returns, he will be revealed from the air, from the God-dimension all around us (Col. 3:4; 1 John 3:2). The Son of Man will "come in his kingdom" (Matt. 16:28). This is why we pray in the Lord's Prayer that he will be King *on earth as he is in heaven*. This is why, according to N. T. Wright, almost everything we believe about the rapture these days is dead wrong.[10] We are not going to float up into heaven to meet a Jesus who is hovering somewhere in the clouds before zipping off into outer space. When Paul writes in 1 Thessalonians 4:4–17 about how "the Lord himself will come down from heaven" and how we "will be caught up together with them in the clouds to meet the Lord in the air," he is not trying to describe how we are going to get vacuumed into the sky. Rather, he is mixing "code, metaphor, and political cartoon," combining the Hebrew story of how Moses "came down" Mount Sinai with Roman political imagery of how a Caesar would return to his capital city. Paul is trying to describe the indescribable. "Jesus will have his 'royal appearing,'" says N. T. Wright, "like Caesar coming back to Rome.... His glad, loyal citizens will 'go out to meet him,' not in order to stay with him out in the countryside, away from the city, but to escort him in triumph and splendor back to his capitol."[11] Someday we are going to welcome Jesus into his fulfilled Kingship. Someday we are going to behold the mixing and blending of heaven and earth that began in Mary's womb and will not be completed until the end. Every day, the earth is becoming more and more enchanted. With every passing hour, God's kingdom draws closer to fulfillment. Jesus is coming. We are going to be a part of it. The whole earth is going to be a part of it. And so we wait, as one betrothed. We wait as watchmen wait for the morning.

Would not conversation be much more rational than dancing?" asks Ms. Bingley in Jane Austen's *Pride and Prejudice*. "Much more rational," replies Mr. Bingley, "but much less like a ball."[12] The modern conversation about the universe rings very "rational." But should we want it to be? Does the night sky make us moderns shiver and feel lonely, or does it wrap us like a quilt, remind us of a story bigger than our own? I used to look up at the lonely and far-flung sky with its ten billion galaxies and distances just short of infinity, and feel like it was playing a practical joke on me. I loathed it. I pretended outer space did not exist. I found *Star Wars* and *Star Trek* movies with machinelike ships floating through eerie voids suffocating. Outer space's shapeless, trackless vastness and its dying stars impressed upon me a glum sense of blank, black inconsequence. "Melancholy space and doleful time," as Wordsworth penned.[13]

To the Christians of yesteryear, however, the starry skies were a colorful carnival, a twirling of planets and stars at a dance party. Watching the night sky was like watching line dancing at a hoedown.

When friars or peasants looked up at the overhanging firmament, they were not looking *at* darkness, but *through* darkness, a darkness like thick cocoa, the kind of darkness that is inherently sweet and warm. The majestically fretted roof was like a vaulted ceiling of a cathedral. They would lie on their backs and try to hear the night music, the songs of worship to God.

Have you ever seen medieval frescoes? Angels fill the heavens, divine speech floods out of people's mouths in scrolls, and halos crown saints' heads. Everything is devilishly dark or gloriously golden with meaning. Marcus Aurelius wished that people would love the universe the way we love our hometowns.[14] That was actually possible in the Middle Ages and all the way back to the ancient Israelites. Their cosmos was a God-bathed cosmos:

> *In his hand are the depths of the earth,*
> *   and the mountain peaks belong to him.*
> *The sea is his, for he made it,*
> *   and his hands formed the dry land.*
> *Come, let us bow down in worship,*
> *   let us kneel before the LORD our Maker. (Ps. 95:4–6)*

Does this psalm express a primitive sentiment? Or does it describe a natural law deeper and truer than the law of gravity?

In order to even begin to taste and savor the world of which the old Christians were connoisseurs, "the last enchantments of the Middle Age,"[15] we must shake off scientism's chronological snobbery, the bigotry against the past. Barfield has, I think, rightly observed that "twentieth-century minds are brought to believe that, intellectually, humanity languished for countless generations in the most childish errors on all sorts of crucial subjects, until it was redeemed by some simple scientific dictum of the last century."[16] C. S. Lewis once penned against this: "The characters of the planets, as conceived by medieval astrology, seem to me to have a permanent value as spiritual symbols — to provide a *Phänomenologie des Geistes*, which is specially worthwhile in our own generation."[17] He described the medieval heavens as "tingling with anthropomorphic life, dancing, ceremonial, a festival not a machine."[18]

Imagine with me, if you will, that you are a medieval monk who has stepped outside to pray. You are lying in the dark, high on a mountain pass, listening to the wind and tree noises or the lonely howls of doglike creatures, and looking up into a lidless sky. There is no light pollution, no sound of distant freeways. Nothing but a small distance of ether separates you from the celestial bodies of the zodiac (a Greek word meaning "circle of animals"). You remember how the Bible says:

> *He who made the Pleiades and Orion,*
> > *who turns midnight into dawn*
> > *and darkens day into night,*
> *who calls for the waters of the sea*
> > *and pours them out over the face of the land —*
> > *the* LORD *is his name....*
>
> *He is the Maker of the Bear and Orion,*
> > *the Pleiades and the constellations of the south. (Amos 5:8;*
> > *Job 9:9)*

You shudder at the thought of having Jehovah ask you, as he did Job:

> *"Can you bind the chains of the Pleiades?*
> > *Can you loosen Orion's belt?*

Can you bring forth the constellations in their seasons
    or lead out the Bear with its cubs?" (Job 38:31–32)

You remember the book of Isaiah:

"It is I who made the earth
    And created mankind on it.
My own hands stretched out the heavens;
    I marshaled their starry hosts." (Isa. 45:12)

You know (because you are a learned medieval monk) that biblically the word *host* carries connotations of living armies or the whole company of heaven. You are not alone. You are living in a universe that has a pulse. Would you not shudder beneath your russet robe? Would you not creep back to your hermitage, all the while glancing back up to the sky with something like awe?

It is true: the way the ancients thought the planets and stars functioned was wrong. But was there willingness to take the best science of the day, limited as it was, and to then sew it into the tapestry of the Christian narrative wrong? What if our universe is valuable, not because it is a story that can be explained, but because it is God's story being ever told? Let modern scientists keep learning how it all *functions*: their discoveries do not likely change what it *means*. We might think, like pudgy and stuffy-minded Eustace in C. S. Lewis's *The Voyage of the Dawn Treader*, that a star is nothing but a giant ball of bright gas. But he is scolded, "Even in your world, my son, that is not what a star is but only what it is made of."[19]

Sometimes that which we cannot see brings beauty and clarity to the story. Quarks and strings are premises in contemporary physics that no one can see and that no one expects to see. Yet they give intelligibility to the whole. For medieval thinkers, God brought meaning and intelligibility to the whole. And if they had known about quarks and strings and a heliocentric galaxy, they still would have thought God is the key to creation. The text of creation was interpreted through the text of Revelation. And so it came naturally to them to integrate science with theology. Even though God is invisible, they were convinced it is God who keeps the planets in their orb and holds the universe together, Jesus who is "sustaining all things by his powerful word" (Heb. 1:3).

And they were right. In Christendom, donkeys can talk because the whole world is resonant with God's words. Every day pours out his speech, and the night sky reveals his knowledge. There is nowhere we can go to escape his voice. Our galaxy's sun moves through God's language as one might dance in a ballroom. The earth is sustained by God's voice, his song. Psalm 19 reads quite explicitly:

> *The heavens declare the glory of God;*
> *the skies proclaim the work of his hands.*
> *Day after day they pour forth speech;*
> *night after night they reveal knowledge.*
> *They have no speech, they use no words;*
> *no sound is heard from them.*
> *Yet their voice goes out into all the earth,*
> *their words to the ends of the world. (Ps. 19:1 – 4)*

The Bible says that God created the stars as "signs to mark sacred times, and days and years," and made the sun to govern the day and the moon to govern the night (Gen. 1:14, 16).

Stars, according to the Bible, can serve as signposts, warning, and encouragement. In the book of Judges, the stars are portrayed as angels who can participate in our lives. After years of Canaanite oppression under the harsh rule of Sisera, the Israelites finally proved victorious because "the stars fought, from their courses ... against Sisera" (Judg. 5:20). The "morning stars sang together" when God created the world (Job 38:7). "He determines the number of the stars and calls them each by name" (Ps. 147:4). Jesus pointed to the stars and warned of the last days when

> *"the sun will be darkened,*
>   *and the moon will not give its light;*
> *the stars will fall from the sky,*
>   *and the heavenly bodies will be shaken.*
> *Then will appear the sign of the Son of Man in heaven."*
>   *(Matt. 24:29–30)*

In Revelation 1:16, Jesus holds seven stars in his right hand. These "seven stars" are sometimes understood to be the seven visible planets, the seven "wandering stars."[20] Christ literally holds our days. Jesus is the Lord of time.[21]

Chapter 16

A God-Bathed World

The God-filled and meaningful pattern of the universe was *presupposed* in the literature and art of the Middle Age, where ancient astrology and Christian theology finally wed. It was a backcloth to the stage of life. It gave shape to the liturgical year of Christendom. To the medieval Christian, there was no such thing as "outer space." They called the luminous promontory of stars the "seven heavens." See the diagram on the following page.

One of my favorite poets, the Anglican priest John Donne, calls them "the Heptarchy, the seven kingdoms of the seven planets."[1] These "seven intelligences" included the Sun (Sol) and the Moon (Luna), Mercury, Venus, Mars, Jupiter, and Saturn. Before Copernicus (AD 1473–1543), the "seven heavens" were not heliocentric but geocentric. So each sphere was a ring that circled the earth. They were like the rings on a tree stump or the levels of a seven-story building. Above and beyond the spheres of the planets was the sphere of the stars, and then beyond that, the Empyrean (the boundary of the *mundus,* the earth, and the beginning of heaven). What was called the *primum mobile* (literally, "the first moving thing") was the outermost sphere that moved around the earth every twenty-four hours, carrying

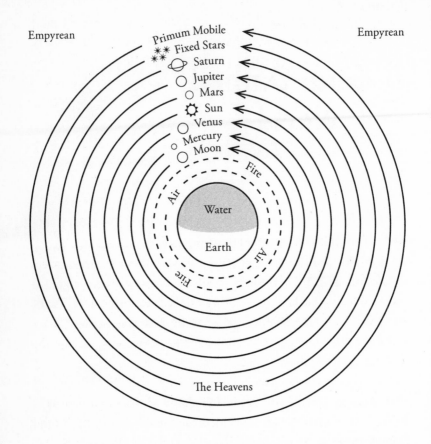

the inner spheres with it. It was known as "the love that moves the sun and the stars."[2] God surrounded the spheres. There was literally nowhere one could go to escape his presence. The heavens were indeed *telling* of the glory of God. The words of a contemporary rabbi beautifully express this old vision: "Creation is the language of God. Time is his song, and things of space the consonants in the song."[3] Christ is, as the medieval monk Odo of Cluny called him, "the Lord of history (*dispositor saeculorum*)."[4]

Created and sustained by God, the planets were resonant with a cosmic music through their harmonious movements. The universe was synchronized in every detail to the unending song of Christ—or as ancient philosophers called it, "the music of the spheres," the *musica mundana*. For Roman philosopher Christian Boethius, the music humans make with instruments is linked to the music of the human soul and ultimately to the music of the spheres.[5] The goal in art, then, is to synchronize with the harmoniously vibrating universe. The only reason you can't hear it is because it's *always* singing. It's ubiquitous. You have never *not* heard it. The idea goes back through Augustine to the Pythagoreans: the universe has a hidden order, a musical harmony, a secret timbre. God is always singing.

Medieval Christians believed they could perceive God's reign in reality.[6] God's existence and supernatural powers were all around them. While humans were comprised of "the four essences," which we'll look at in just a minute, the stars and seven planets each inhabited a sphere made of an ethereal transparent fifth element called *quintessence*, "the fifth essence." It was thought to compose the heavenly bodies and to be latent in all things. The planets affected the character and fate of people by their *influence* (Latin *influere*, "to flow in"), which courses through the earth's *atmosphere* and through the *ether* in people's arteries.

As long as it did not lead to idolatrous worship, and as long as it wasn't used for profit, the medievals approved of and even incorporated astrology into their scientific inquiry and theology. Theologians were strongly opposed to determinism, the idea that our fortunes are written indelibly in the stars. But they did believe they could influence us, kind of like how we today believe in seasonal affective disorder, that sunlight changes our moods. The concept of the seven spheres affecting the human body was the medicine of the day. For example, if a medieval doctor were to be stumped as to why his patient was sick, he would thus attribute it to "the influence of the air," which is where we today get our word *influenza*. Though never responsible for people's actions, the planets could nudge them toward vice or virtue, insight or insanity, lust or love, even idolatry or worship of Christ.

These planetary spheres, the great celestial wheels, glowed with charismatic personalities that warmed or cooled people, events, plants, and the metals couched in the earth's crust. Their influences would move through the earth's exhaled breath, the *atmosphere*. "The dynasts seven incline from heaven and literally fill the air."[7] Thus Homer wrote beautifully of the influence of Orion:

> *Thro' the thick gloom of some tempestuous night*
> *Orion's dog (the year when Autumn weighs)*
> *And o'er the feebler stars exerts his rays;*
> *Terrifick glory! for his burning breath*
> *Taints the red air with fevers, plagues, and death.*[8]

The four elements—earth, water, air, and fire—were believed to fill the human body as well as the surrounding air.[9] Because each element lined up with three of the signs of the zodiac, it was through these four elements the planets would ray down their sweet influence. The human body was said to contain four *humors*, or "moistures," that were in relationship with the atmosphere: blood, phlegm, bile (or choler), and black bile (melancholy). Depending on your mixture, you could be *choleric, melancholy, phlegmatic*, or *sanguine*. This is why we still say to this day that someone can have a good *temper* or a bad *temper*, be good *humored* or bad *humored*. Diseases, or "distempers," were also connected to the mixture of these humors. Medievals believed, with the ancient Greek Hippocrates, that spirit (from the Latin *spiritus*, "breath," "life") flows through our arteries. This "spirit" was also known as *animal* (Latin *anima*, "soul"), and *ether* (from the Greek *aither*, "the upper air"). Thus, for Hildegard of Bingen, and for many others, man was a microcosm of a macrocosm, a tiny picture of the whole universe.[10]

Depending on the *disposition* of planets at a child's birth, that child could grow to be, say, *jovial*, *saturnine*, or *mercurial*. If a child was born under Saturn, that child would be predisposed to melancholy; if Venus, amorousness. The child would be in *sympathy* or *sympathetic* to a given planet. Most of us today use words like *disposition* or *sympathy* completely unaware that we are using astrological metaphors. My friend Oliver tells me that the Hebrew word *mazel* means "sign" or "constellation." So when Jews say "Mazel tov!" (another way of saying, "Congratulations!"), they are really saying, "May you have good stars!"

In making sense of the celestial dance, Christians in the Middle Age smuggled from the Egyptians liberally. To them, the pagan gods that governed the seven intelligences, the seven planets, were symbols of the one true God. God created the planets, and so they reflect God's attributes (love, sovereignty, beauty, power, and so on). Thus God also created seven "spirits" (angels, gods, deities, intelligences) to govern the seven planets. This is why when you look up into the beautiful dome in the church of Santa Maria del Popolo in Rome, you see the divine forms of the planets with an angel hovering over each, while over and above them all, in the round central aperture, God the Creator raises his arms in benediction and command. Made by the Christ himself, these created planetary deities reflected certain attributes of their Creator. As humans were subject to the planetary gods, the planetary gods were subject to the one true God. Thus, fifteenth-century astrologer-poet Lorenzo Bonincontri wrote, "In the beginning, the Almighty Father, in order to rule the world by laws, set high in the sky the stars and the globes of the planets. He gave them numbers and names, and assigned to them such a nature that everything would be determined at definite times. Through them he shaped the morals of men and their bodies, and their whole fortune, accidental happenings, man's life and his ultimate day, sequence of his fate, end of his labors."[11] Although the theology and science of such a vision is dubious, I think the idea that the stars are not dead masses, but auxiliaries of agents of Jesus' love and intention for us is a step in the right direction. The spiritual world is then inseparable from the physical.

Even the days of the week were governed by the spheres, the planetary gods. It's a tradition we maintain to this day:

Sunday is named after Sol (the Sun).

Monday is named after Luna (Moonday).

Tuesday is named after Mars (Tyr was the Norse equivalent of the Roman Mars).

Wednesday is named Mercury (Wodin was the Norse equivalent of the Roman Mercury).

Thursday (Thor was the Norse equivalent of the Roman Jupiter).

Friday is named after Venus (Frigg was the Norse equivalent of the Roman Venus).

Saturday is named after Saturn.

If you want to learn more about the personality or influence of each of these planetary deities, I strongly recommend reading C. S. Lewis's *The Chronicles of Narnia*. The literary scholar Michael Ward has connected the disparate dots of Lewis's seven fairy tales to the seven corresponding planetary spheres.[12] For example, *The Lion, the Witch, and the Wardrobe* expresses the planetary influence of Jupiter.

Have you ever wondered why Santa Claus is in Narnia? It's because Jupiter (Jove) is "cheerful and festive; those born under Jupiter are apt to be loud-voiced and red-faced."[13] Who better captures the rouged, round, and jolly character of Jupiter than Santa? He is the bringer of gifts, laughter, and merriment. Since Jupiter is a kingly planet, that's why Aslan, the lion king, arrives in this book. Aslan is the Christlike, Jupiter-like king of Narnia who has the power to make Peter and Edmund kings and Susan and Lucy queens.

In the Old Testament, Melchizedek is a priest-king who is said to be an early resemblance of Christ himself, according to the letter to the Hebrews (5:5–10). Like Christ, Melchizedek is especially associated with bread and wine (Gen. 14:18–20; cf. Luke 22:19–20). Fascinatingly, the name Melchizedek means "My king is righteousness." Ironically, one meaning of the name "Jupiter" is "righteousness." To ancient astrologers like the wise men who visited Bethlehem, Jupiter was the chief of the Roman pantheon. Jupiter was known to pre-Copernican astronomers as *Fortuna Major*, the Greater Fortune, sovereign of the seven heavens. Positioned between hot Mars and cold Saturn, Jupiter is a temperate, magnanimous planet. Jupiter was the celestial symbol for leaders and gods.[14] His metal is tin, the shine and sturdiness of which, before the canning industry, was considered splendid, royal. He is masculine, moist, airy, and sanguine. He is associated with the lion, eagle, ox, peacock, and dolphin, and with strong stags, kind elephants, thrones, mighty oaks, apple trees, pleasant weather, north-westerly and northeasterly winds, palaces, courts, castles of pomp and solemnity, and feasts. He is the bringer of halcyon days, heartsease, prosperity, and joy: "Winter past and guilt forgiven."[15]

When all the cold and biting winds of winter are washed away by the spring rains, and the heartsease and joy of summertime are in full bloom, that is when Jupiter is about. He has a commanding aspect, a handsome shape, a ruddy complexion, a high forehead with soft, thick, brown hair, and a beard.[16] His laughter is like the blare of loud trumpets, his whisper is like banners waving in the wind, and his tears are like crashing waves. C. S. Lewis encouraged his readers to imagine Jove's kingliness as a king at peace in the Great Hall, rosy cheeked, with a bold face and fearless aspect, fat and happy.[17] His angel is Zadkiel, the archangel of freedom and mercy, and the patron angel of all who forgive. In Jewish rabbinical tradition, Zadkiel is said to be the angel who prevented Abraham from sacrificing his son, Isaac.

Jove rules over the clergy, the higher orders of law students, and crafts of wool. His influence on mortals is merriment, temperance, and good cheer. In Dante's *Comedy*, just and discerning princes go to Jupiter's sphere. Festal Jove represents a time of peace and joy, when "winter is past; the rains are over and gone" (Song 2:11). When poorly received, Jove's influence can make people become common cheats and drunkards who, though careless and improvident, will never entirely lose the good opinion of their friends. They will be the butt of many jokes.

To the naked eye, Jupiter is a brilliantly white gleam. The planet is still cooling down from its formation, and the heat fuels the planet's dazzling clouds and strong magnetic field. Seen through a telescope, its nonsolid surface displays ever-changing shades of brown, tan, yellow, orange, and blue-gray. All the inner planets of our solar system are rocky and small, but from Jupiter on out, the planets are large and gaseous and command their own moons and rings. The planet has a slow gait; it takes twelve earth years for Jupiter to orbit the sun, which means that it spends about a year passing through each constellation of the zodiac.

For medieval Christ-followers, then, Thursday is a day to remember that we are in the service of the High King whose kingdom is extremely nigh. The day reminds us to reflect on how God's glory is reflected in mighty oak trees, strong lions, and gentle elephants. Whatever is kingly, priestly, and festal, whatever is Santa-like, whatever is lion-hearted, whatever is golden, gentle, and good, think on these things.

I 'm not into horoscopes or astrology. But I am a lot less proud than I used to be. I mounted my imaginary donkey to pursue equestrian adventures only to find that it is I who have been the ass. Modernity has made a fool of me. "The gods' presence in the world goes unnoticed by men who do not believe in the gods."[18] I have been like Balaam. I've been blind to the life of God around me, too proud to look under rocks or through a telescope in search of something spiritual. It never occurred to me that the cherubim and seraphim and demons and God himself are everywhere. "You are right as right can be," gasps Sancho, the stout squire in Cervantes' *Don Quixote*, "and I am an ass — though I do not know why I am talking about asses."[19]

No, I am not into black magic or horoscopes, but I am into making room for God to make a clean sweep of our lives. I want to know, serve, and delight in Jesus Christ. I want to resemble him. And when I look at the world around me, I want to see the joy and love of the Trinity that it reflects — in the planets orbiting the stars, in the tides and seasons, in a pregnant woman, in atoms and molecules. I want to enter into the dance of the cosmos that Christ set in motion when he made it. And I think the medieval synthesis is a helpful tool for cleaning house, for putting everything in its proper place before God.

I think it is this coloring, this poetic significance that Balaam the scientist misses out on. I'm not asking you to believe any of it. I'm only asking you to appreciate its beauty and its imaginative value, to savor the aroma. In doing so, we might learn by way of delight how to approach and appreciate our world. The change of mood is subtle, but it makes all the difference.

Chapter 17

The Love That Moves the Stars

Today we could very likely hear someone say in a bored and matter-of-fact way, "If you shake an apple tree, apples will fall out," as if the one idea naturally leads up to the other. But under the old vision of the cosmos, people could say with Joshua, "Shout and blow trumpets, and Jericho's walls will fall over." They did not say it, however, as if it were a necessary fact, an obvious effect of a cause; to them it was a marvel, a thing to behold. They would not have imagined their theory about the connection between trumpets and falling walls to be a fixed law, the way contemporary people imagine the connection between shaking an apple tree and apples falling to be unquestionably a law. For the medieval mind, theories were only efforts to save the appearances, not solid facts. But contemporary people, at least when it comes to shaking apple trees and falling apples, "feel that because one incomprehensible thing constantly follows another incomprehensible thing, the two together somehow make up a comprehensible thing," as G. K. Chesterton observed. "Two black riddles make a white answer."[1]

Is it any wonder we moderns don't believe Balaam's donkey could talk? Our cult of facts and laws leaves no room for mystery or magic, no room for God.

Christendom invites us to be joyful in the *wonders* of creation. But creation is not wonderful if we pretend it is sensible. If we regard a donkey as an obvious thing, good only for heaving and hauling, we cannot wonder at it. "Have you journeyed to the springs of the sea or walked in the recesses of the deep?" God asked Job. "Have the gates of death been shown to you? Have you seen the gates of the deepest darkness? Have you comprehended the vast expanses of the earth?" (Job 38:16–18). "This simple sense of wonder at the shape of things," wrote G. K. Chesterton, "and at their exuberant independence of our intellectual standards and our trivial definitions, is the basis of spirituality.... To draw out the soul of things with a syllogism is as impossible as to draw out Leviathan with a hook."[2]

The idea of seven harmonious spheres revolving around the earth is no longer believable. We now know that our solar system twirls on the outer edge of a spiral galaxy. Advances in instrumentation have helped us spy two more planets, three if you include Pluto (it was dubbed a "dwarf planet" in 2006). Uranus was discovered in 1781, Neptune in 1845. We now know these planets revolve around the sun, which is not a planet but a medium-sized, medium-aged star. Our moon is Earth's satellite, not a planet. In one way, the medieval cosmos is not true. But in an even bigger way, it is true. It is correct in assuming that there is no division between things natural and supernatural, in taking Jesus at his word that the kingdom of God is at hand. Everything is connected; nothing is left out. People did not always perceive themselves as "objects" poking at an "environment," but as creatures in creation. How could they? The solar system coursed through their veins; influenced their fates; shaped the seasons of planting, harvest, and fallow time; and gave form to their worship. They were a part of it.

When medieval persons reasoned, they *participated* in a divine reason that came to them through the created order. To our ancestors, meaning came from *outside* the person. It was *outside* cerebral biochemistry. In other words, knowledge was a gift; it was borrowed currency. This is why, for example, to the medieval mind, no one could *be* a genius. "Genius" comes from the same word for *genie*. A genius was the attendant spirit present throughout someone's life, like a guardian angel ("demon," a person's patron spirit, is the old Greek form of the Latin *genius*). The poet was believed to be "possessed" by a god or angel who would give utterance through his mouth. Thus our word *inspiration* (*inspirare*) means "to breathe, or blow into." This *inspiration* was breathed through the poet only as and when the muses chose and only at special times and places. This is why writers have been notoriously picky about the places they go to "invoke" the muses. To retire to one's study or to stroll with pen and paper was to climb Mount Parnassus, home of the muses. Sometimes they were silent, but when they sang, the poet lost himself to the divine wind.

So, too, did the theologian surrender himself in prayer to the Holy Spirit. So, too, did doctors and students of the natural sciences seek knowledge *as a gift*. In the third century, Plutonius was convinced that "the arts do not simply imitate what they see (in Nature) but reascend to those principles from which Nature herself is derived."[3] Genius comes from outdoors. To *discover* is to uncover or reveal. To *invent* is to find. So medievals did not believe people were the creators of truth, beauty, and goodness; they believed people could only find it, uncover it.

But then modernism turned thought inside out. We turned our gaze from the cosmos inward, to the personal human being. We became less and less a part of creation and more and more the spectators of our "environment."[4] This detachment, although it indeed has roots in Platonism and Aristotelian thought, was foreign to medieval doctors and laymen. Atomlanders now speak of *Nature* when medieval thinkers would have used the word *God*. "From where then does the ability to create art arise?" asks Edward Wilson. "Not cold logic based on fact. Not God's guidance of Milton's thoughts, as the poet himself believed. Nor is there any evidence of a unique spark that ignites such genius as is evident in *Paradise Lost*." Wilson concludes that inspiration comes from "the biologically evolved epigenetic rules that guided them."[5]

Modernism also gave way to a new and glorified perception of the self, self-confidence and self-awareness. Words that used to describe the outside world became expressions of the inside world, words like *aversion, agitation, constraint, disappointment, dissatisfaction, embarrassment,* and *excitement*. People began to think genius came from within rather than from without. They began to think what was right was right because they thought it was right, as if they were the standard and means of truth. Even reason, remember, cannot be reasonable if it is the result of random electrons changing over time. The individualism of modernism has left us with nothing but ourselves to trust.

This is what is so important about the medieval synthesis: it understood that truth does not come from within ourselves; it comes from *outside* ourselves. Though truth fills the cosmos, it is a truth bigger than the cosmos. They did not believe they invented truth and meaning; they discovered it. They built communities and tended toward wonder and worship. Over the shouting peasants, creaking and rambling oxcarts, braying donkeys, and clattering pots and pans, the medieval ear could hear the hum of a universe singing God's praises.

Until scientists become critical of their discipline's own theoretical foundations and develop an epistemic theory adequate to the nature of God's creation, they will endlessly defer the question of truth. For all the medievals got wrong on a pragmatic level, their Christ-centered posture toward knowledge, their epistemic discipline, is commendable to us. For them, learning about everything from the human body to the planets in our galaxy was a way to believe better and to love God more.

For the Christian, the ultimate truth is found in Christ Jesus (John 14:6; 17:17–19; Rom. 15:8). He has given authority to the church to bear witness to him (Eph. 4:11). But how does the church find what is true and then assimilate it in order that they might proclaim it with authority? In Scripture, it is impossible to consider truth (ἀληθεια, *aletheia*) apart from God's steadfastness, his providence and redemption.[6] Truth is not an abstract value, but the living salvation story of Jesus Christ, the Son of God and son of Mary. We discover truth, therefore, not only through intellectual processes, but through repentance. "Truth is not what we think and say, but what God has done, will do, and is doing," wrote Karl Barth.[7]

We might baptize every good and useful human thought into the story of God unfolding, from the belief in Jove to the belief in the atom, but without love for Jesus it will be almost worthless. For Christians, epistemology is really Christology: Jesus shapes how we know. The whole world becomes intelligible through the incarnation, wherein humankind might enter fellowship with him in whom all things are summed up and in whom all things are redeemed.

When the way we know is also the way we love, we open ourselves up to the possibility of wisdom (*sofia*); we begin to enter God's character in Christ, "in whom are hidden all the treasures of wisdom and knowledge" (Col. 2:3; cf. Rom. 11:33; Eph. 3:10; James 3:17). He is, to quote the old poet again, "the love that moves the sun and the stars."[8] When we enter the love-bathed world that the cross of Christ opens to us, nothing—absolutely nothing—can escape God's epic salvation story. It is written across the skies, and it is written on our hearts.

You might be asking where, exactly, all this is going. Why have we been clip-clopping around the medieval cosmology on a donkey and looking up at the stars? What does any of this have to do with our modern world, a world of Dr. Dre–endorsed headphones and adventure shoes, a world of Oscar Mayer wieners and nylon tents. What do the scrolls and hand-bound books of ancient Christianity have to offer a world crowded with Facebook requests, huge LCD Wi-Fi HD TVs, and an endless stream of text messages? We can learn from them. They teach us how to believe better. Learning to delight in the old cosmos equips us better to understand our world and our lives in the trail of the incarnation.

Part 5

The Sanctification of Time

In Which our donkey hobbles to a stable in Bethlehem. A pagan prophesies Jesus' birth, and pagans use astrology to find the Messiah. Old church bells ring. Liturgy and the church calendar can make our daily life a nonstop prayer. We begin to enter God's time zone.

"Arise, shine, for your light has come,
      and the glory of the LORD rises upon you."

—Isaiah 60:1

O Lord and Ruler of the hosts of heaven,
God of Abraham, Isaac, and Jacob, and of all their righteous offspring:
You made the heavens and the earth, with all their vast array....
All the powers of heaven sing your praises,
and yours is the glory to ages of ages.

—Prayer of Manasseh

Chapter 18

The Yule Log Burns

Did you know that the Puritans very nearly made Christmas extinct? They considered the raucous partying, gluttonous eating and drinking, and ale-drenched cheer of the Christmas season too earthy and pagan. In 1643 the English parliament even outlawed the observance of Christmas. For twelve sad years, Christmas passed by in England without music or dancing, feasting or drinking. When the *Mayflower* sailed to America, it brought with it this puritanical, anti-Christmas sentiment. In 1659 the general court of Massachusetts ordered a Christmas ban, fining anyone who celebrated Christ's birth five shillings. Thank God, the ordinance was repealed in 1668, and the Yule log burns again.

Most historians agree that Jesus was not born on a cold Judean winter night. So why do we celebrate Christ's birthday on December 25? The answer lies in the winter solstice, the shortest day of the year, which falls around this day. In ancient Babylon, the feast of the son of Isis (goddess of nature) was celebrated on December 25. It was a day of great merriment and gift giving. In ancient Rome, they celebrated Saturnalia, a holiday honoring Saturn, the god of agriculture. Soon after, on the first day of January, they observed the Calends of January, which celebrated life's victory over death. During this season, bands of costumed singers called mummers traveled from house to house entertaining their neighbors. Today we call it caroling.

Meanwhile the pagans of northern Europe celebrated their own winter solstice, which they called Yule. Yule means "wheel," their symbol for the sun. On December 25 they celebrated the birth of the sun god, Mithras. As he grew, the days became longer and warmer. Mighty Yule logs were burned in his honor. Holly berries were the choice food of the gods. Mistletoe was also a sacred plant, and the custom of kissing under the mistletoe began as a fertility ritual. Evergreen boughs represented fertility as well, and for this reason they were often present at weddings. Evergreen trees were brought into homes during the cold winters as a reminder that soon their crops would grow again. In this dark season, it was the custom to light candles to encourage the sun god to be reborn.

In a uniquely Mars Hill moment in 350, Pope Julius I declared that Christ's birth would be celebrated on December 25. Christ was the true Sun, who died and was reborn, the true Creator and Sustainer of the universe. He was the real thing of whom the neighborhood gods were only shadows. Thus the pagan Romans could baptize, as it were, their ancient feasts into the true feast of Christ. The earliest record of decorating an evergreen for a Christian celebration was in Germany in 1521.

Should it bother us that Easter Day, the principal feast of the church year, is named after Eostre, the Teutonic goddess whose name is associated with springtime, growth, and fertility? Is it okay that Christianity wandered into Greco-Roman antiquity and German folklore, incorporating pagan myths into its traditions and calendar? Is it okay for Chaucer and Spencer and Milton and Donne and Shakespeare to use classical gods to describe qualities of the one true Trinitarian God?

Before we cringe at the mentioning of medieval Christianity's earthy-spiritual calendar, their "gods" and "goddesses" and "magic," we must remember that Atomland has its own gods and magic and calendars. They're just secularized, materialistic gods and calendars. The modern idea of how everything in the universe works is one of medicine, shopping malls, the autonomous self, and machines. No magi at the feet of Jesus. No star shining in Bethlehem. No miracles.

But the medieval church was not magical because it was full of peasants who lived in ignorance, misery, and superstition. Jolly, squalid old Europe was magical because it believed Jesus was Lord of *all* things, not just *some* things. Even magical stars. Even pagan gods. Even Aristotle and the Pythagorean theorem. Even Roman and northern European cults. Paul even says in his letter to the Romans that it is through the seasons and the stars and the harvests and the trees that we can know God. "For since the creation of the world God's invisible qualities — his eternal power and divine nature — have been clearly seen, being understood from what has been made, so that people are without excuse" (Rom. 1:20). This is because the world is the Lord's and everything in it. *Heathen*, we must remember, originally meant "of the heath," and *pagan* originally meant "of the country," a "rustic." In the literature and art of Christendom, "the gods are God incognito and everyone is in the secret."[1]

Christmas is a time when we remember when the whole universe aligned and God became a man. Around the world, Christians light candles, wrap presents, gather around lighted Christmas trees, and sing praises to the newborn Jesus. We retell the ancient story of Mary and Joseph and the miraculous birth of our Savior. We marvel at the angels who sing to shepherds and at the star that led the magi to the manger. The birth of Jesus is a joyful thing, a childlike thing. And this is why, despite years of advertisement and sentimentalism, Christmas remains a feast day for jesting, gaiety, the carnival, the festival—a day for celebrating the arrival of the King.

Chapter 19

A Star in Bethlehem

In the doldrums of December, Minneapolis is caked in a deep layer of snow that mutes the city noises and frosts the housetops. Traffic is horrible. The streets are filled with a slushiness that never seems to go away. It can get so cold it hurts to breathe. I actually like when the mercury drops (if you can believe it). I find a strange satisfaction in scraping ice off my windshield. I love the flannels and the boots and long johns. When winter is nipping at your heels and the forecast is threatening snow, the local menu is packed with stouts, browns, and bocks to sip. The shops are full of fresh-cut evergreen bows and carols. I even love Santa and Rudolph and all the other reindeer.

This year, however, I tried to sweep away the straw that covers our usual nativity scenes to expose a floor we forget was there. Everything about the Christmas story — from the incarnation to the wise men on their camels — clearly illustrates coherency of creation and the unity of knowledge in Christ, and in a way I never would have thought. Here we see what looks like God himself plundering Egypt when he caught the attention of pagan astrologers using a star.

When I brushed aside the wrapped presents and the modern

...ns, I discovered not only manure, cherubim, and sera-
...in, but the zodiac etched across the floor, which really bothered me
at first, because I'd always associated astrology with hippy voodoo, the
occult, and cheesy horoscopes in the backs of magazines. But when we
saddle our proverbial donkeys and trek back into the dark forests of
history, it can be very helpful to think of astrology more like the way
we think of astronomy today. Historically, astrology is just another
branch of science, "the study of the stars." In fact, it is the origin of
science itself.

Imagine a longstanding community of Persian astrologers called
magi scanning the skies, generation after generation. What kind of
celestial aberration would have been unique enough to grab their attention? What could have compelled these well-to-do scholars to under-
take a dangerous and difficult journey to the boonies of Bethlehem?

The answer lies in Balaam and his talking donkey. Remember
the Moabite king who summoned Balaam to curse the Israelites? His
name was King Balak. There are many parallels linking the story of
King Balak and Balaam to the magi's visit. King Balak hailed from
the same homeland as King Herod's family. Balaam thwarted Balak's
plans to destroy the Israelites, just as the magi thwarted Herod's plan
to destroy Jesus. Balaam spoke of a star symbolizing the birth of the
Messiah, just as the magi spoke of a star announcing the birth of the
King of the Jews.

In Numbers 24:16 – 17 Balaam prophesied that the Messiah
would be revealed by a regal star:

> Decree of Balaam son of Beor,
>   decree of the man with 20/20 vision,
> Decree of the man who hears godly speech,
>   who knows what's going on with the High God,
> Who sees what The Strong God reveals,

> *who bows in worship and sees what's real.*
> *I see him, but not right now,*
>> *I perceive him, but not right here;*
>> *A star rises from Jacob*
>> *a scepter from Israel. (MSG, italics mine)[1]*

Christians have always believed that a celestial event revealed the birth of the Christ, and for thousands of years, it has been believed that Balaam's prophecy foretells the messianic star. We read in the gospel of Matthew: "After Jesus was born in Bethlehem in Judea, during the time of King Herod, Magi from the east came to Jerusalem and asked, 'Where is the one who has been born king of the Jews? We saw *his star* when it rose and have come to worship him'" (Matt. 2:1, italics mine).

It is not likely that a star would shine "directly above" the manger in Bethlehem. It is also not likely that the magi followed a comet, because back then comets (*cometai*, "long-haired stars") were thought to forewarn disaster, typically the death of a king. Matthew's word for the star was the Greek *aster*, "star."

The universal acceptance of astrology is attested to by the fact that these astrologers were permitted to have an audience with a king and that they did not *ask* King Herod if a king had been born but audaciously (and dangerously) *informed* the king that some other king had been born. What's even more noteworthy is that Herod believed their tale of a regal star in Judea's constellation without question. When Herod heard their observations, "he was disturbed, and all Jerusalem with him" (Matt. 2:3).

If, like me, you don't know much about astronomy, this might be difficult to follow. When the magi said, "We saw his star when it rose," they would have been referring to the heliacal rising of a star or planet as it first became visible in the sky. In Hebrew, the word for

"East" also means "the rising." Matthew 2:1 would be better translated, "We saw his star *at its rising*." Jupiter, a kingly planet, aligned with Aries (which was the constellation of Judea) in the springtime, when the prophesied Jewish messiah was to be born. So the Magi traveled west as they followed "a star in the East." These Persian astrologers followed the portends and clues of the astronomy of their day straight to God Incarnate.

Should we flinch at this? Did a *star* really shine over Bethlehem, over Jesus the prophesied Messiah? Like Balaam, these astrologers were pagans. They were the first Gentiles to adore Jesus, and we celebrate God's glory in their story every Epiphany. Are we really to believe that a pagan's prophecy about celestial omens came true in the incarnation of Jesus Christ and that pagan astrologers used astrology to come and worship him? Some insist that God does not use outside (sinful or secular) resources to accomplish his will; moreover, Atomland says creation is a dead, lifeless blob. But Scripture is packed with references to God not only creating and sustaining creation, but employing it in his good service. And if God can use Pharaoh, a flood, famines, and frogs, God can speak through anything—from donkeys to the planets—and use anything from science to mythology to bring his plans to fruition. All truth is God's truth, even if it comes from an unexpected place, like Balaam's blessings and prophecies.

Picture Jesus lying in the manger when he was just a baby. As God and swaddling clothes snuggled in that food trough, the bold aroma and earthy sweetness of animals, hay, humans, and God in one room entwined. God and natural ingredients in perfect harmony. The whole universe aligned. Even the stars were a part of it. The project that Jesus started when he spoke our universe into existence was beginning to come to fruition. The prophecies, the stars, the virgin birth: they all were weaving the tale of redemption. When God became incarnate, the whole universe was involved, even the stars, even pagans who had not yet heard of him.

> *O star of wonder,*
> *Star of night,*
> *Star with royal beauty bright*
> *Westward leading, still proceeding,*
> *Guide us to thy perfect light.[2]*

Chapter 20

In the Year of Our Lord

As far as I can tell, it is this unity, the divine and worldly synthesis of the stable in Bethlehem, that the incarnation so radically brings into focus. The incarnation sets the conditions for miracles and talking donkeys, a world rich with meaning, and salvation stories. When I read the Christmas story, I am constantly reminded that the whole earth *really does* groan because of our sin; nature *really is* eagerly waiting for God's plans to come to fruition in us (Rom. 8:19–22). The incarnation, God becoming man, constantly reminds us we cannot be gnostic dualists, people who believe that matter is bad and the spiritual is good, and the two are never combined. Christ combines them. He combines them in Genesis, and he combines them in the incarnation. The physical world is good enough for God because God made it. He *became* it. We cannot think that the body or God's creation is bad.

God's creation is beautiful, really. Even the stars are a part of God's plan. They are, rather, signposts and witnesses to his manifest glory. "For since the creation of the world God's invisible qualities—his eternal power and divine nature—have been clearly seen, being understood from what has been made, so that people are without excuse" (Rom. 1:20). I used to think Paul meant something like

"God's beauty shines in the sunsets." But I am beginning to understand that what this verse really says is that God has invisible qualities that he reveals to all men and women, not just Christians, through his visible creation. Everything that has been made bears his mark, his original stamp of approval. "The earth is the LORD's, and everything in it" (Ps. 24:1). God is so evident in creation that we have no excuse for *not* stumbling upon him.

In reference to the dates before and after the birth of Jesus, most of us Christians do not flaunt the usage of BC and AD like Christian imperialists. We simply believe that Jesus is the Christ of God and that he is the Creator and Sustainer of time. All history is either leading up to Jesus or pointing back to Jesus. The Christian calendar dates everything around the moment of Jesus' incarnation, because Jesus is what history is all about. This is why Christians insist on saying things like "in the year of our Lord Jesus Christ" instead of the sleek and "neutral" turn of phrase, Common Era. Christ is the Lord of *all* things, not just some things. He fills our time. Time exists because God exists. He is the reference point. *Anno Domini*. In the year of our Lord Jesus Christ.

In his letters, Paul says the phrase "in Christ" more than fifty times—we are to live in Christ, rest in him, thrive in him. Jesus reorders our history, our calendars, our daily planners. As a Christian, then, believing that Christ changes everything about the universe and human history, the reckoning of years forward and backward from Christ makes perfect sense. The calendar is Christendom's ontological statement about the universe, then. Though we might not always be able to see the "big picture," we can live our lives assured that the story of the whole world is pointed toward "the day of the Lord" or "the kingdom of God." In the triune God, history has meaning and direction.

My friend Oliver tells me that the Hebrew concept of time was that it is a divine reality. As the ancient Jews despoiled Egypt, they transformed agricultural festivals into spiritual holidays. Passover was originally a spring festival, beginning on the first full moon after the vernal equinox, but for the Israelites it became a time to celebrate the exodus from Egypt. The old harvest festival at the end of the wheat harvest, the Feast of Weeks, became a celebration of the day on which the Torah was given at Sinai. The old festival of vintage became the Feast of Booths to commemorate the dwelling of the Israelites in booths during their sojourn in the wilderness.

God's story of redemption was interwoven into the cycles of nature. Passover and the Feast of Booths, for example, also coincide with the full moon. In the Old Testament, *qadosh* means "holy." It is used for the first time not to create a holy mountain or a holy temple or a holy spring but to sanctify time: "And God blessed the seventh day and made it *qadosh*" (Gen. 2:3). In the Old Testament, the holiness of *time* precedes the holiness of *space*.

The medieval Christian idea of time builds on an old Jewish idea of time. We read in Genesis that God made the world in six days, and on the seventh day he "rested." This does not just mean that God went on vacation. For six days, God made the heavens and the earth for his own enjoyment. On the seventh day, when he had finished the job, he moved in. *Creation* is God's temple, a place in which he lives. Thus, from the Jewish point of view, the Sabbath is not a day for laziness. It is a chance to savor time from a different perspective, to get human time into God time. It is a day to put the busyness of daily life second and to put what history is all about into relief.

The Sabbath was a sign, then, a reminder that God's purposes for creation are worked out in time. The Sabbath was a living promise that God would be faithful to his people, that time was pointing to something, getting ready for someone. For the Jews in the Old Testament, this anticipation was heightened by the larger rhythm of Sabbaths, in which every seventh year, the Year of Jubilee, slaves would be set free and debts canceled, and laborers could rest. And Jews in Jesus' day were anticipating the "seventy weeks," the seventy times seven years, the Jubilee of Jubilees, when they would be free (Dan. 9:24). The whole world was spun out of a series of sevens — seven-day weeks, seven years, and seven times seven years (half centuries). This is why Matthew artfully arranged Jesus' genealogy in three groups of fourteen generations. In the opening of his gospel, we read six groups of sevens before the final seventh, the Sabbath of Sabbaths moment in time: the incarnation. This is why Jesus inaugurates his ministry in Mark 1:15 with the words: "The time has come." Jesus was announcing the Jubilee.

You know how Jesus was always breaking the Sabbath regulations? It's not because they were legalistic and Jesus was antilegalistic. It's because the Sabbath was a signpost pointing toward God's promised future. When Jesus healed on the Sabbath or walked through grain fields on the Sabbath, it was not to make a statement about the law, but to express that all the Sabbaths, all the sevens, had come together in his ministry. He was *the* moment, the new creation, the healing and feasting Sabbath itself, the fulfilled time that all of history had been waiting for. Jesus is a living, breathing, joyous Sabbath. He is "Lord ... of the Sabbath" (Mark 2:28). He is Lord of time.

Echoing Judaism, medieval Christianity became patterned around the holiness of time. Every castle had an attached chapel; every occupation, a patron saint. The calendar was a collage of festivals and saints' days. The Christ story was notated, like a beautiful piece of music, and this patterned song has rung from the belfries and steeples of Europe for nearly two millennia. Since the sixth century, bells were the most popular public timepieces of the Western world. Churches and monasteries rang their bells, calling the faithful to pray; the sound filled the villages and hamlets. Our word *clock* comes from the word for bell in medieval Latin (*clocca*).

When my great-grandmother Inez traveled Europe, she wrote of these same church bells ringing as late as 1962. She recorded in her journal, dated June 7: "We had tea in the little village inn to see 'how they do it' in a little German town. The 'town crier,' with his news broadcasts from the center of town over the loudspeaker many times a day, was interesting. The ringing of the church bells periodically through the day was beautiful—and in the evening it was a longer period." She also wrote, "The German expression *wunderbar* is used so much to express pleasure or beauty." *Wunderbar* is where we get our English word *wonderful*.

The liturgy of the church became a way to tell time for ordinary life. Tertullian was the first to require that Christians pray at the third, sixth, and ninth hours of the day, and Benedict codified seven precise times for prayers as a part of the liturgical day of his monastic order. They were known as the Divine Office, prayer times that became the canonical hours:

1. *Matins* ("morning") just before daybreak
2. *Lauds* ("praises") at dawn
3. *Prime* ("the first hour") just after daybreak, at 6:00 a.m.
4. *Terce* ("third hour") at 9:00 a.m.
5. *Sext* ("the sixth") at midday
6. *None* ("the ninth") at 3:00 p.m.
7. *Vespers* ("evening") at 6:00 p.m.
8. *Compline* ("contemplation") after sunset

The call to pray was announced by church bells, which punctuated the day for not only the monks but the townsfolk. Time was sacred, an arrow pointing to God.

I can't help but wonder if the early saints were that far off. We might have cell phones and Dr. Dre–endorsed headphones and adventure shoes, but we can't escape the fact that we live in our galaxy. We are still in thrall to the heavens. The Delphic adage "As above, so below" is in at least one sense true: our experience of time still hinges on the moon, the sun, the earth, and every planet swirling around in our solar system, each a tiny part of the whole—each, therefore, having some tiny effect on our experience of time. The earth dances around the sun, drawing the four seasons in its train, 365 days from one point to any other, composing our year. It spins our days around its axis. So much of what makes up our lives is bound up in our twenty-four-hour day, the sun and the moon. It takes Earth twenty-four hours to rotate completely around its own axis and roughly 365 days to circle the sun—but try to imagine life on a planet like Mercury, where it takes fifty-nine days to rotate around its axis. That's six weeks of baking sunlight followed by six weeks of freezing darkness.[1] Our efforts to bring order to our lives, to work with the seasons, to enact our religious beliefs, are based on the planets. The solstices, when the sun reaches its northernmost and southernmost positions in the sky, inaugurate summer and winter. The equinoxes, when the sun stands betwixt the solstices and the length of night and day are equal, usher in spring and autumn. Orion warns of a looming winter, and Leo promises that winter will pass into spring. The Pleiades blow in the first autumn breezes. The planets' cycles are mysteriously, and yet not so mysteriously, connected to every part of our lives.

This is why Christians have almost always and everywhere developed a liturgy, a way of living and participating in the heavenly song. It's a way to return to the cosmic dance, to stop making everyone and everything orbit around us but to allow ourselves to orbit around Christ. Liturgy helps us join the goodly fellowship of the saints in having personal peace and forgiveness and bringing *shalom* to the whole world.

Liturgy is as old as the apostles. Our word *liturgy* comes from old words for minister (λειτουργός, *leitourgos*) and public service, worship of the gods (λειτουργούς, *leitourgia*). These meanings, well known and used by the early church, come from an even older word combination of "public" with "working" (λειτος, *leitos*, and ἔργος, *ergos*). Liturgy is a person's role in a community, especially a religious one, a person's public work. Liturgy, then, is the corporate worship officially organized by the church, offered by the priestly society (1 Peter 2:5), and available to the members of a church, the "body of Christ" (1 Cor. 12:27). Liturgy means "public work," and this translates into Latin as *officium*. Thus, when we go to work, we say we are going to "the office," and when we pray together, we pray "the office." It was the way to live in thrall to God's cosmic story, his project of restoration. Even the stars have a liturgy.

The other night I went on a long walk. My mind was full of thoughts about monks singing cantillation and Christmas and the swirling planets and the Holy Spirit. Lights shone from the shops and houses onto the drifting snow. The sky was dark and leaden. Everywhere spirals of chimney smoke were violently snatched by a biting wind and blown through the streets of Minneapolis. The arctic air was stinging, but the smell of wood smoke, like wafts of myrrh or incense from a thurifer's swinging censor, was reassuring. When you are grateful for the little things, they become big things.

As I walked past thigh-high snowdrifts, I thought about how

Christendom changes something as common as the calendar into a road map, inviting us to live the life and passion of Jesus. December becomes Advent, a time to prepare for Christ's coming. When the darkness couldn't be greater, Christians celebrate the birth of Jesus, the Light of the World. January becomes Epiphany, a time to remember how Jesus made himself known to Gentiles, the magi. March becomes Lent, a time to confess our sins and to prepare for commemorating Christ's death on the cross. With April and springtime, we tie the greenness and new life of the season to Christ's new life. We enter the season of Holy Week to remember Christ's suffering, which culminates in Easter, the day we celebrate Jesus' resurrection. June is a time to celebrate Pentecost, the birthday of the church. These are the seasons spun naturally out of God's historic activity on earth. In Christ time is not a dead, godless idea, but a divine reality.

I wondered, *If we are going to reorder our lives around Jesus, perhaps one of the most practical ways we could start would be to do what the medieval Christians did as they went about the serious living of the faith.* They reordered their calendars differently. In Christendom we celebrate the feast days of the saints, the holidays that retell the biblical narrative. Good Friday is our Memorial Day. Pentecost is our Independence Day. When we believe that Christ is the unity of knowledge and the coherency of creation, we keep our stories in God's story. We begin to enter God's time zone. We become so much more than observers. We become participants.

Every day we wake up on the tail end of a story that has been unfolding for millennia: history and culture, geology, genealogy, the whole cosmos, and God. The Christian calendar invites us to escape the straitjacket of individualism and pluralism, and instead to get our orientation and sense of self in this larger story. The liturgical year gives us a comprehensive context by which we can see all of God's creation and salvation stories in the light of Christ. God wants not only to save souls but also to care for and cultivate the earth, to restore and renew the whole universe.

Since we have chosen to live the life of the Spirit, we get to do so much more than just entertain ideas in our heads or swoon over sentiments in our hearts. We get to work out God's plans, his good intention and plan for us, in every detail of our lives. When we live the historic liturgy of the church, we reenact the gospel of Jesus. We wear it like a garment. We make it our daily sustenance. What we *know* about God and what we *do* about God become a single knot. Living the Christian calendar puts each of us in a place to take responsibility for doing our creative best to grow in Christlikeness, to enter the generous common life of the saints. Liturgy creates the context for us to work for the benefit of all, starting with the people closest to us in the community of faith and spreading out into the whole world.

Part 6

You Are
What You Eat

In Which Winston and Rose are introduced. Blood is a real atonement. God's covenants are more real than the law of gravity. Mr. Potato Head is considered. Sacraments are how we can be re-membered into the body of Christ. Baptism and the Lord's Supper are a foretaste of our home in God.

In Christ we, though many, form one body, and each member belongs to all the others.

—Romans 12:5

This oneness [of the church] derives from the stability of God and is welded together after the celestial pattern.

—Saint Cyprian, *The Unity of the Church*

Chapter 21

Deep Magic

I used to wish I could find a word to describe the participation in the divine life, the way we can join God in his redemptive work on earth, how we can enter God's time zone. For a long time, I called the way the apostles Paul and John saw the world "miraculous" or "enchanted" or even "magical." But then I discovered that Christendom had coined a word. The word our Christian ancestors used to describe how the world is sacred and heavy with significance is *sacramental*.

Sacraments are where the resurrected Jesus' engagement with our world comes home to roost. Christ-followers of yore said there are unique places that make humanity's participation in the God life palpable, that bring the sacramental world of Jesus into focus. They call them *sacraments*, the unique intersections where humanity crosses with God. Somewhat like the doctrine of the Holy Trinity, which is an idea not explicitly referred to in Scripture but a doctrine that emerged in early Christian theology, the idea of sacraments became a teaching and practice of the early church teased out of Scripture but fully expressed by the church fathers over the first five hundred years of church history.

Sacraments are revelations of God's presence, outward and visible carriages of inward and spiritual activity. They are focal points of the love of God. Although the whole world is *sacramental*, only a few special intersections are *sacraments*. For the church fathers, another word for sacrament (*sacramentum*) was mystery (μυστήριον, *mysterion*) — expressing the idea that the world really is charged with the grandeur of God and that this glory spreads out in bursts of activity through Christ's church. Although God's presence and abiding love permeate creation, it cannot be tasted, smelled, touched, or seen directly because God transcends human comprehension. We cannot comprehend God with our minds or our five fallible senses, and thus they remain, always, a mystery.

You know how when you adjust the lens on an old camera it brings the picture into focus? What was blurry becomes clear. That's what exploring the Eucharist and Baptism — the two sacraments instituted by Jesus — is like. The Eucharist, especially, brings our journey through enchanted, covenantal Christianity into focus. Prayer was the unifying theme of medieval Christendom, and "the Mass" (an old-school nickname for the Lord's Supper) was the highest form of prayer. Here we stumble upon the full intersection of miracles, the coherency of creation, the implications of the incarnation, and the repercussions of the resurrection. Paul and Luke write about how the Lord's Supper is "a new covenant." Covenants are what C. S. Lewis might call the "deep magic," or the "strong magic."[1] Deep magic is not some empty custom that assists intellectual habits. To participate in the Eucharist is to participate in the love of Jesus and his universal church in a real and transformational way. We become a *communion*, a living covenant.

And so after about four score and seven trinitarian breakfasts and nearly two hundred whiffs of C. S. Lewis's pipe smoke, my holy pilgrimage lead me straight to the center of enchanted Christianity: the

Holy Eucharist. If you could spread out a map of all there is to reconnoiter of Christendom, you would find that we have covered only one tiny freckle on a vast and daunting landscape. But we are about to take a sharp right turn into the "Middle Earth" of Christendom: covenant, the Lord's Supper.

Chapter 22

Dinner at Winston's

"Do you soak your beans?" Winston asked.

"Um, yes. Yes, I do," I said, taken aback.

"I just love to cook a pot of beans," Winston sighed as he walked into the kitchen.

Every first Sunday of the month, Winston and his kind wife, Rose, have me over for dinner. As a bachelor who subsists on too much frozen pizza, I am more than obliged to join them. Winston has an irresistible southern charm and four kids, all of whom are the happiest, brightest, and most well-mannered rays of sunshine. Besides being our church deacon, I think Winston has one of the best jobs in the world. He's a sommelier, a wine connoisseur, and a journalist. He travels the globe drinking and writing about wine. I don't know how he landed the gig, but restaurants seem to care what he thinks about vino, and they pay more than a penny for his thoughts. The goofy thing is, he has a low, almost salt of the earth attitude about the kitchen. He just loves to cook, and he can't stand pomp. On more than one occasion, I've caught him stirring something fragrant—or flagrant—while sneaking swigs from a magnum of red wine. I for one like to play sous-chef when I'm in his kitchen, helping with the chopping, opening cupboards, and igniting burners like a burgeoning Ratatouille.

I followed Winston into the warmly lit kitchen, his two enormous Great Danes close behind. Outside, the houses of Minneapolis were frozen like ice cubes in a tray. The kids were making snowmen in the backyard, and Rose had run to get fresh sourdough bread. Winston does all the cooking in the house. Rose says she won't touch a saucepan for all the gold in the United States Treasury.

Winston grinned. "So, what do you think of the cuisine?"

"Well, now … ah, what do you think it might be?" I asked. He had said it was a hearty minestrone stew, but as I peered into the voluminous pot, all I could see was an assortment of bones and vegetables and mystery parts.

"Come on. We're not talking frozen chicken cordon bleu here," Winston laughed with southern flair, stirring the soup with a long-handled spoon.

"So you've been thinking about individualism and secularism, you say?" he asked, picking up the conversation where we left off in the living room. He set a cast iron griddle on the stovetop and looked up at me.

"Right," I said, sitting on a barstool. "Scientism not only separates humanity from creation and people from their own souls, but it also separates us from one another. Staunch materialism seems to go hand in hand with a severe individualism." I told Winston that I had been reading how the scientific revolution shaped Enlightenment values of individualism because it celebrated the power of the autonomous human mind, the ability of scientists to come to their own conclusions, rather than defer to authority. The idea that people could rule themselves, master their own fates, and re-create their own identities became increasingly popular. Now, the worldview of Atomland praises autonomy and independence while disparaging our interdependence and creatureliness.

"But there's something about being a Christian that means you are no longer just you," I concluded. "You can't keep living for yourself or doing your own thing. You become part of the whole story of the church. You are brought into the body of Christ himself. Your life is no longer about you."

"I like to remind parishioners of that," said Winston. "It isn't very helpful to talk about God's redemptive plan for the world in terms of how *I* am saved or how *I* have a personal relationship with Jesus. True as that may be, the Bible says we are all being sanctified together, as a community, as one body. 'For we were all baptized by one Spirit into one body,'" Winston quoted from 1 Corinthians, raising his wine glass.[1]

"Whatever this oneness is," I said, "it's incarnational. I mean, you have to live it. And when you live it, you enter the community of Christ that is not bound by space and time. We join the saints and martyrs of the past in the eucharistic feast."

"Exactly," he said, setting another saucepan on the stove with a bang. "That's why I always say something supernatural happens at the Lord's Supper. As individual members of Christ's body, when we Christians eat and drink the body and blood of Jesus, we do way more than remember. We are *re*-membered," he said. "Think of Mr. Potato Head. It's like we're put back together again. Every Sunday morning at the Lord's Supper. Every Christian. One big potato."

Now, there! I thought. *There's an idea I can sink my teeth into.* The fading afternoon light poured through the lead-paned windows of their old house.

"The last loaf at the store!" said a jubilant Rose as she stomped through the back kitchen door. I gulped when I saw her round belly protruding out of her winter coat. She was nearly eight months pregnant. Winston smelled the bread and gave her a triumphant kiss.

"Rose, my joy and my crown, you pick a fine sourdough loaf!"

"Not that I was in a rush, mind you," clucked Rose, grinning and turning toward me. "My husband has no concept of time in the kitchen. When he says dinner'll be ready in fifteen, I'm calling the kids an hour later."

Eventually, the kids came in from the backyard smelling of wet socks and sweatpants, and there was a flurry of hand washing, cleaning up, and preparing for supper. The kids laid out the silver, and Rose set vases brimming with dried wildflowers on the table. Eventually we all sat down to a loud, delicious meal.

After the plates and glasses were cleared, and after Winston and I did more than a sink full of dishes, we sat in worn reading chairs in the living room. A low fire burned on the hearth, warming the winter drafts.

"I'll just have more of that Cabernet," he said, helping himself to a large second. "It's none too popular these days," said Winston, waving his glass, "but I think the wine is important, and I think something supernatural happens when the priest consecrates the elements, something covenantal," he continued, standing up to add a few logs to the fire. "These days folks think covenants are as meaningful as continental breakfasts. But the Eucharist is more than a snack or a symbol. It's a sacrament."

"Explain," I asked, leaning back.

"Yessir. Remember that duck crossing sign down by Lake Calhoun? It has a picture of ducks on it so that we'll slow down. No one would say the road sign mysteriously participates in duckness, magically joins in the quacking and swaggering ducks found around Uptown. That symbol and real live ducks are two completely different things. But if that road sign were a sacrament, it would be so ducky that drivers would be afraid the sign itself might swagger across the street. The road sign and ducks would not be completely separable."

I was trying not to laugh at Winston's duck metaphor, but nodded in agreement.

"You see, when Jesus spoke in parables, he was using symbols, not instituting sacraments," Winston continued. "In saying the kingdom of God is like mustard seeds, he wasn't saying the kingdom of God is *inside* mustard seeds. But in that Upper Room, Jesus said the bread and the wine *are* his body and blood, and then told his disciples to eat and drink as both a remembrance *and* a covenant. A covenant is a relationship and commitment between God and his people, Tyler. It's not only natural but supernatural. Like you say, it's something lived."

"But some people think a miraculous Lord's Supper is superstitious," I countered.

"Not any more superstitious than believing that saying a few lines of the believer's prayer somehow gets Jesus into your heart," Winston pointed out. "Miracles are more than just the prayers we pray or the water we baptize with or the cup we drink. It's what God does *through* them that counts. Like most things in God's kingdom, the Lord's Supper is not only *information*, but *transformation*."

We listened to the fire. I couldn't help but think about all the Christians who used to burn each other at the stake over this very issue. They should have been sitting around with a few bottles of Cabernet, talking it over in prayer.

"I wonder why so many of us *want* the Eucharist to be only a symbol and not also a sacrament," I mused after a moment. "The modern gut reaction is to recoil when we hear about things like incense, holy water, talking donkeys, or a supernatural Lord's Supper. Maybe this is one example of how a lot of us have unmiraculous, secular presuppositions. We still live in a world created by man, not God."

"It breaks my heart," my good friend said with shining eyes. "The incarnation and the resurrection must not have really sunk in for them. How does the blood of Jesus save wretches like you and me if blood is always meaningless?"

Rose came in with cookies.

"You ain't talking about *blood* again are you honey?" she moaned.

"Yes, ma'am," said Winston, smiling.

"My dear boy," she said, patting me on the shoulder before quickly exiting.

"I've been studying wine my whole life, Tyler, but ever since I came to know Jesus as Lord, it's blood that's fascinated me."

"No kidding?" I said dryly, not sure if I wanted to hear about it.

"When Jesus died on our behalf, it was not an abstract gesture, you see. His blood was a real atonement. The Bible says blood must be spilled for the remission of sins. It talks about how Abel's blood cried out from the ground. Blood gets splattered over the doorposts of the Israelites. It's sprinkled all over altars in the Old Testament. You can hardly read a page of the Bible without pickin' up the idea that blood must be shed for sins. Christ had to not only die, but *bleed* on the cross."

I squirmed.

"Yessir," Winston said plainly. "Jesus' blood—the actual plasma and erythrocytes and leukocytes and platelets that circulated in his arteries and veins—is 100 percent necessary for the sacrificial atonement of our sins."

He was right, of course. The Bible has weird ideas about blood. It is part of Christianity's deep magic. This deep magic has nothing to do with wands and broomsticks, but with the blood covenant between God and his people. It is frightening to remember that, in its old meaning, *to bless* means "to consecrate with blood."[2] It is frankly disconcerting that Christianity is a religion of blessing, a cult centered around blood rites: blood before the mercy seat; blood offered as atonement on the sacrificial altars of Abraham, Isaac, and Jacob; the blood of Christ offered for us on the cross; the blood we drink at the Lord's Supper. As one member of Oxford University's literary group The Inklings put it, "One might almost say that wherever the blood is involved, the Lord is involved.... Without the shedding of blood, there is no remission of sins."[3] The apostle Paul said clearly, "For God was pleased to have all his fullness dwell in [the Son], and through him to reconcile to himself all things, whether things on earth or things in heaven, by making peace through his blood, shed on the cross" (Col. 1:19–20).

"But it's beautiful," Winston continued. "God became human. Our Creator has human blood coursing through his veins. This is why the blood of Jesus draws us up into a deep and intimate connection with God." The fire was crackling and shone in his eyes. "This is why when I receive the eucharistic bread and wine, the wine Jesus says is his blood, I just cannot deny that something miraculous happens, something about blood and covenant and the mingling of God and people."

"A deep magic, a covenant, sealed in the blood of the Lamb and kept alive in the Lord's Supper," I added.

I set my glass of wine on a stack of *Southern Living* magazines and closed my eyes. Sitting with Winston by the fire, I felt like I was in a novel. We could hear Rose running the children's bathwater upstairs. The Great Danes beat the floor with their tails. With a warm rush of feeling, I realized that all of this—the food, the children, the love that filled this household—was a tiny picture of the kingdom of God.

If the Lord's Supper is not an empty ritual, but a living participation in the body of Christ, a stepping into an old covenant and blood rite, I wondered why so many of us Christ-followers take it so lightly. I thought it was probably because we've spent too much time in Atomland and not enough time wandering the old-growth forests of Christendom. I thought about Winston and his companionable wife and kids and all the wine he had in his cellar. I thought about the love that fills their home, and how it must be something like a foretaste of the kind of home we'll find in heaven.

Like having a family and children, the Eucharist summons us to a scary reality that requires something of us. And when you approach it in light of the medieval synthesis, you begin to appreciate that there really is a cloud of witnesses, a company of saints. The church really is a mystical communion. We're all linked and connected in Jesus. Even the stars and planets are involved. And the Lord's Supper is where this comes into focus.

"You're mighty quiet. Do you know something I don't know?" Winston asked.

"God became man so that we wretches might become one with God," I almost whispered. "Jesus shares our nature so that we can participate in God's nature. This is what amazing grace is all about, Winston. Since the beginning, God's plan has been to bring all things—the stars and the world and people—together in him. It's hard for me to wrap my mind around, but God really loves us. We are living a salvation story."

"Welcome to God's country!" he said with bright eyes.

Chapter 23

The Spell to Break the Spell

Winston is right to focus on the covenantal quality of the Lord's Supper. While lumbering around on the four mostly obstinate legs of an ass, I was fascinated to discover that after that most mysterious and appalling episode where Balaam's donkey talked to him, Balaam honored God's covenants with Israel. This international magic expert pronounced oracles that alluded to the great covenant made to the patriarchs: that God had chosen Israel to be his chosen people. He noticed that Israel was not only blessed but had the very presence of God in their midst. He was deeply moved that God was not a distant vassal lord but a king who lived and reigned among them. Bravely, then, this non-Israelite prophet sought to be blessed as the children of Abraham were blessed, and acknowledged another promise made to the patriarchs: "May those who bless you be blessed and those who curse you be cursed!" (Num. 24:9).

Balaam divined that Israel was different from other nations, that they were distinct—did not "consider themselves one of the nations"

(Num. 23:9). And while prophesying that Israel would enjoy prosperity and protection, Balaam reaffirmed the covenantal promises made to the patriarchs. Beginning in Genesis 12:1–3, God promised Abraham three things: land, descendants, and covenant relationship. Thus Balaam's first oracle mentions Israel's unique relationship with God and the nation's great population. His second oracle celebrates Israel's covenant relationship with God. The third and following oracles predict Israel's future peace and prosperity in the Promised Land, the rise of the monarchy, and victory over foes. The promise of a future king is a rarer but important element in the patriarchal promises, and Balaam's fourth vision describes this future king. Three times God promised the patriarchs that "kings shall come from you" (Gen. 17:6; see 17:16; 35:11).

Balaam then gave a prophecy about "the days to come," which can also mean "in the final days." That he was speaking of the distant future is further endorsed by the beginning of his oracle: "I see him, but not now; I behold him, but not near." He continued: "A star will come out of Jacob; a scepter will rise out of Israel" (Num. 24:17). Although his predictions were partially fulfilled in the reign of David, whose victories over the Philistines would prefigure Jesus' victory over sin and death, these prophecies are about the coming Messiah. The reference to the king and the star give strong eschatological, priestly, and messianic overtones to Balaam's last oracle, which we looked at in part 5.

As I looked past the long ears of my donkey, I discovered that covenants are what the whole story of Balaam and his crazy ass are pointing toward. God's loving covenants with humankind are the truest things on earth. They are a deeper magic than the law of gravity or the rules of arithmetic. They surpass all understanding. Nothing is deeper or wider. Covenants are unique relationships that God makes with his people as he acts in history, and they are at the heart of enchanted Christianity's dark forest.

Traveling even further back into the recesses of historic Christianity, I discovered that covenants are always marked with a sign. God made a covenant with Abraham that through his offspring blessings would come to the earth, and he gave Abraham the sign of circumcision (Gen. 17:11). After God led the Israelites out of Egypt, he made a covenant with them of which the Sabbath was the sign (Ex. 31:13). But the sign of the new covenant instituted by Jesus and sealed with his blood is the Lord's Supper. Thus, Christ says, "I confer on you a kingdom, just as my Father conferred one on me, so that you may eat and drink at my table in my kingdom" (Luke 22:29). What the Old Testament calls covenants, the New Testament calls the kingdom of God. Covenants are what kings make with their subjects. Covenants and kingdoms are different ways of talking about the same thing. To enter the kingdom of God is to enter a covenant where God reigns over people and creation.

The biblical narrative is chock-full of God's saving promises, his covenants. Together they weave a tapestry of salvation rich with magic and meaning. After sin entered the world, the Lord pledged that he would save his people, starting with the promise that the seed of the woman would triumph over the seed of the serpent (Gen. 3:15). In his covenant with Abraham, God pledged his people land, seed, and a life of blessing. The Mosaic covenant guaranteed blessing if Israel obeyed the Lord, and the Davidic covenant promised a great king would be born in the line of David, and that through him the promises originally made to Abraham would become a reality. What we call the "new covenant" promises that God will give his Spirit to his people and write his law on their hearts so that they will obey his will.

Christians believe that Jesus, Joshua the Christ, is the fulfillment of all God's saving promises. The deep magic, the covenants of the Law and the Prophets, are realized in Jesus. He is the Messiah who sits on the throne of David forever, the Prophet predicted by Moses. Indeed, he is the new Moses, declaring God's good news as the true interpreter of the Mosaic law. He is the new Joshua who gives rest to his people. He has the authority to forgive sins, and it is he who becomes the sacrificial Lamb on the altar for our sin. The blood the Israelites once painted on their doorposts to be spared from the angel of death finds fulfillment in the cross; thus the blood of Jesus covers the doorpost of the whole world. And this generous salvation, this overarching paschal blood covenant, was instituted by Christ himself in that upper room at the Last Supper.

Just as the old covenant prefigured Christ's new covenant, so too did the Passover prefigure the Lord's Supper. This is why Paul wrote, "Christ, *our Passover* lamb, has been sacrificed" (1 Cor. 5:7, italics mine). Interestingly, it was on the eve of Passover that Christ first invited the disciples to participate in his body and blood, which would date the crucifixion to be on Passover itself, the same day as the killing of the Passover lambs, and this reckoning would enrich the nuance of Christ's becoming the true Passover.[1] In the Eucharist, Jesus invites the faithful to share in his "Passover" from death to life, from corruption to incorruption, from weakness to strength, from ignominy to glory.

The Lord's Supper is the spell that breaks the spell. Atomland turns people into observers in an environment, but the Eucharist tells us of what better, truer story we are a part, a covenant story in which donkeys talk and the world is held together by that "love that moves the sun and the other stars."[2] Origen says that the church is "the cosmos of the cosmos,"[3] and Saint Cyprian says the church is "welded together after the celestial pattern."[4] Christianity invites us into participation with the planets and the stars, the earth, one another, and God. We are creatures in creation, and the Eucharist summons us into living membership in the family of God. The bread and wine are a tiny sacrament that involves us in Christ's unfolding story, the story of deep magic and covenant, the story of the heavenly spheres.

Last Sunday I was at church, and I took a moment to look around. So many children, old people, couples, and singles — so much diversity — and God is fitting us together, brick by brick, stone by stone. We are no longer strangers or outsiders, as Atomland would have it. We are in God's home country, and we *belong* here. We are the beautiful house of God, all of us built into it, towering high and strong. When we are living in covenant with God, we are living in harmony with God's salvation plans, his plans for the world at large.

And so every Sunday when we celebrate the Eucharist, ordinary people like Winston, Rose, and me are retelling God's salvation stories. We are slowly becoming a living Eucharist.

We live in a covenant cosmos. Since Christians are in a common relationship with Jesus, members in his family, we are all heirs of the covenants Balaam referred to when he blessed Israel. We are among Abraham's descendants. Now we are able to receive God's life, just as Abraham received it. When God made the universe, he was establishing his kingdom, and even though the catastrophe of sin has broken and marred it, the good things of this world constantly invite us into his presence. The Lord initiated redemption through choosing Israel to be a light to the nations through covenants that pointed to the coming of the King, and in the coming of the King — in the incarnation, sacrifice, and resurrection of Jesus — redemption has been accomplished. Ever since then, the mission of the church has been to spread the news about the King and to continue the messianic feast.

In a world where donkeys can talk and planets swirl through the thick love of God, sacraments signify Jesus' cosmic restoration. All of creation will someday be restored to its original purpose, which is to glorify the triune God. The whole world, even ourselves, is a gift received from God and to be offered to him for his glory. And this gratitude for our creation, preservation, and salvation in Christ is expressed in the Eucharist, the "thanksgiving."

Baptism and the Lord's Supper restore modest things like water and wine and bread into the covenant with God they were meant to be, the kind of covenant that will come to completion when the ripple effect of God's covenants at last brings all of creation into consummation with Jesus. The baptismal water and the Eucharistic bread and wine are a foretaste of our home in God, a foreshadowing of what we will all someday be in heaven: agents of God shining brighter than the stars.

Chapter 24

Re-membering

It has always floored me that Jesus *knowingly* gave his body and blood to people who were about to betray him, deny him, and doubt him. He gave the bread and the cup to Judas and Simon Peter and Thomas. Jesus knew that the church would not be a museum of saints but a hospital for sinners. And from the beginning, the Lord's Table has always been a school where men and women learn to crucify the old self and to live the resurrection, to love the Lord with all our hearts, bodies, and minds, and to love our neighbors as ourselves. We slowly learn to think in terms of "Adam," the whole human race, instead of just ourselves.

The narcissistic idea that salvation is only about "me and Jesus" is not biblical. In Atomland, human autonomy and individual sovereignty are the basic building blocks of the good life. In Christendom, however, radical autonomy is a sin that amputates the believer from the corporate body of Christ. When we are born again, we no longer think in terms of "me, myself," but in terms of all humankind, of Adam.[1] Only when we begin to see ourselves in terms of "Adam" instead of "me," will we begin to understand what happened with the incarnation and what happens at the Communion table. Only then will we become actually (and not just metaphorically) intimate with Christ. The church comes from Christ's side, just as Eve was taken from the side of Adam: this is why the Venerable Bede described Christ and the church as sharing "one nature."[2]

This is what theologians call "the doctrine of recapitulation," which is just a fancy way of talking about how we are "re-headed" (*re*, "again" + *caput*, "head"). Do you remember the vexed matter of Saint Denis I mentioned in part 1? He was commissioned to convert the people of Gaul and did such a good job that the local pagans got angry and beheaded him. But Denis simply picked up his head, kept on preaching, and became the patron saint of headaches. This re-heading is kind of like what happens when we participate in Communion. The idea is that as heirs of Adam's sin, we were, so to speak, beheaded, decapitated. We are "the broken rung in the ladder of created being," wrote Dorothy Sayers. "The Incarnation is a new glory given to mankind; but that glory belongs to the act of God and not to the nature of man."[3]

We were severed from God in the sin of Adam, but in Christ, the new Adam, we are re-headed. When we were born, we were born into the "guilt incurred, grace wasted, and glory lost" of Adam's fall.[4] But when we are born again, we leave the body of the old Adam and enter the body of the new Adam. We leave the fallen, sinful, headless human race and are "born again" into the church of God, the body where Christ is the head. The Eastern Orthodox term for recapitulation is *theosis*, the "in-Godding" of humankind. Thus, in the second century, Irenaeus described salvation as the "recapitulation" of humankind.[5] God became man and, by doing so, lifted man up into God.

When we were baptized, we became members of Christ's body. This is why when we remember his death and resurrection in the Eucharist, we are "re-membered" into the eternal body of Jesus and his church. When we eat the bread and drink the cup, we are put in a place for God to recapitulate us, to "re-head" us.

I like Winston's way of putting it. Apart from Christ's family, we are like the broken off and lost parts of Mr. Potato Head — random ears, eyes, shoes, hats, and noses. But Jesus puts each of us back together in him. We get re-potatoed.

The eucharistic feast leads to talk of other things that affect the soul: love, loss, sickness, and success. A pattern of life centered around the Lord's Supper changes the whole community of Christians, opening new ways for them to allow God to transform and renew daily life.

You are what you eat," wrote Augustine. He believed that celebrating the Eucharist brings us into intimacy with Jesus and those around us who are collectively Jesus' body. When we share the body and blood of the Lord, we are united not only with the head of the body but also with every member of the body of Christ. This is the whole point of the Lord's Supper, and this is why we call it "Communion." Augustine invites people to the Lord's Supper, saying, "Receive what you are." And when we share the body and blood of Jesus, we commit ourselves to live as the body of Christ. "If you are his body and members of him," Augustine wrote, "then you will find set on the Lord's Table your own mystery. Yes, you receive your own mystery.... Be what you see, and receive what you are."[6]

In other words, we don't just sit around like Winnie-the-Pooh on his stump and "Think, think, think." God demands that we *eat* bread and *drink* wine, because they are like the burning bush or talking donkey. The incarnate and resurrected Christ is uniquely busy and attentive in the consecrated bread and the wine. Jesus said, "Whoever eats my flesh and drinks my blood has eternal life, and I will raise them up at the last day" (John 6:54).

As I hobbled through this old terrain on a twitchy-eared donkey, I was delighted to find that Irenaeus battled the gnostic opinion that the physical world is evil. In his magnum opus, *Against Heresies*, he reminded his readers that Christ was a man, a man who said that real, earthy bread and wine became his actual body and blood:

> For we offer to Christ his own creatures of bread and wine, announcing consistently the fellowship and union of the flesh and Spirit. For as the bread, which is produced from the earth, when it receives the invocation of God, is no longer common bread, but the Eucharist, consisting of two realities, earthly and heavenly, so also our bodies, when they receive the Eucharist, are no longer corruptible, having the hope of the resurrection to eternity.[7]

Let me put this question to you: if the humanity of Jesus never rose from the dead, how can human people enter communion with the risen Christ? If we approach the Eucharist as *only* an intellectual recollection, without any real physical and spiritual communion with God and one another, it follows that the elements of bread and wine are not necessary and we have fallen into the heresy of separating the physical from the spiritual, or worse.

The Lord's Supper is not a game of disembodiment for spooks and phantoms. It is not mental jump rope. Before the eucharistic bread and wine communicate an idea or lesson, they communicate directly to the body, as food and drink, as nourishment. They are a very concrete reality: bread and wine tasted and digested.

It is with great weight that Christ says, "Do this" (ποιειτε, *poieite*— which is plural), not to one person, but to several people. The consecrated bread and wine are to be *shared*. Paul wrote: "Now you are the body of Christ, and each one of you is a part of it" (1 Cor. 12:27). Earlier in the same letter, Paul said, "Is not the cup of thanksgiving for which we give thanks a participation in the blood of Christ? And is not the bread that we break a participation in the body of Christ?" In the Eucharist, the church experiences community, togetherness. He continued, "Because there is one loaf, we, who are many, are one body, for we all share the one loaf" (1 Cor. 10:16–17).

The word Paul used for "participation" (κοινωνία, *koinonia*) translates into the Latin *communio*, which is where we get our English word *communion*. Participating in God's new community, the "communion of the saints" (κοινωνία της έκκλησίας, *communio ecclesiae*), is the big idea behind the Lord's Supper. This is why the old-school phrase "to communicate" means to partake of the body and the blood of Christ *corporately*, to have "Holy Communion."[8] This is why Christianity is not so much an intellectual change or a change in worldview but an invitation to join a people set apart, a community who corporately *lives* the gospel of Jesus Christ.

By the time of Athanasius, the Lord's Supper was understood in terms of *syntax*, how things are arranged so as to be together. "Just as this broken bread was scattered upon the mountains and then was gathered together and became one," prays one of the oldest prayers of Christendom, "so may your church be gathered together from the ends of the earth into your kingdom."[9] One cannot help but think about how horribly wrong are e. e. cummings's lines:

who pays any attention
to the syntax of things
will never wholly kiss you;
wholly to be a fool[10]

For it is by the coming together and partaking, the "syntax and kissing," that we are made whole, wholly fools in Christ.

Cyril (313–386) continued to invite the newly baptized to receive the bread and chalice with faith: "Contemplate therefore the bread and wine not as bare elements, for they are, according to the Lord's declaration, the body and blood of Christ; for though sense suggests this to thee, let faith establish thee. Judge not the matter from taste, but from faith be fully assured without misgiving, that thou hast been vouchsafed the body and blood of Christ."[11] I can almost hear Winston raising his glass and saying with a southern twang, "Amen!"

Chapter 25

Dying with Christ

A sacramental view of the Lord's Supper is not mere hocus-pocus. When the priest invokes the Holy Spirit upon the eucharistic bread and wine (what is called the "epiclesis"—from the Greek ἐπικλησις), there is no "abracadabra." It is a grace that is being received. God does the work. This is why it is called the "Lord's Supper," not the "Christians' Supper."[1] This is also why Augustine said that Baptism "belongs to Christ regardless of who administers it."[2] Or, as Cyprian put it, "Water alone cannot wash away sins. . . . There is no baptism without the Holy Spirit."[3]

A "sacrament" is an outward sign of an inward and spiritual *grace*. All grace comes from God. Any enchanted or miraculous understanding of what it means for us to be the body of Christ must be understood in Pauline terminology as a real "participation." The church fathers believed that where the church is, there is the Spirit of God, and that wherever there is the Spirit of God, there is the church, and every kind of grace. "Where two or three gather in my name," said Christ, "there am I with them" (Matt. 18:20).

When Jesus prayed, "that all of them may be one, Father, just as you are in me and I am in you" (John 17:21), he was not inventing a warm and fuzzy metaphor. He was establishing a solid fact—a fact that the Holy Spirit breathes into being, not us. This unity—what Christendom calls "catholicity"—is not something we bring about, but something to which we must submit. This *koinonia*, this communion-by-participation, invites us into the story of God, outside of which there is no life.

Jesus spoke of this in his eucharistic foreshadowing: "Unless you eat the flesh of the Son of Man and drink his blood, you have no life in you.... For my flesh is true food and my blood is true drink. Those who eat my flesh and drink my blood abide in me, and I in them" (John 6:53–56 NRSV). *Abides* is a powerful verb for Jesus to associate with the bread and the wine. When we come together at the Lord's Table, we join God personally and collectively. He "incorporates" us into himself. In the words of Augustine: "For a man to eat this food and to drink this drink means to abide in Christ and to have Christ abiding in him."[4]

This incorporation begins with death. To enter the old-growth forests of enchanted Christianity, to become truly "re-membered" into the church body, begins with dying to our old self and being raised up with Christ. To participate in the *Corpus Christi*, the body of Christ, "we always carry around in our body the death of Jesus, so that the life of Jesus may also be revealed in our body" (2 Cor. 4:10). "You died," said Paul, "and your life is now hidden with Christ in God" (Col. 3:3).

The kingdom life begins with death. In order to be reborn into the new Adam, we must first die to the old Adam. "I have been crucified with Christ and I no longer live, but Christ lives in me," Paul wrote in Galatians 2:20. And of Baptism, he said, "We were therefore buried with him through baptism into death in order that, just as Christ was raised from the dead through the glory of the Father, we too may live a new life" (Rom. 6:4). We learn with every tasting of the body of Christ (a body that the grieving Mark bitterly describes as το πτωμα, *ptoma*, "a corpse")[5] to die so that we might be reborn with Christ's risen body—Christ and his body, the church catholic. "Whoever wants to be my disciple must deny themselves and take up their cross and follow me" (Mark 8:34), said Jesus.

"Take up your cross," bids our Savior; "Do this in remembrance of me," commands our God. "We were buried with him through baptism into death." This invitation to *communion*, this bidding to join our Lord in his dying—and to eat and drink his body and blood as a means of identifying with his passion—shepherds us into "one bread, one body."

This is the mirth and meaning of Christendom's cosmology. In the Lord's Supper, we can uniquely see that the fellowship of the kingdom is "at hand." It does not stop at the Table. It spreads out, like drops of wine on a napkin, making us of one mind, one in sharing goods, one in carrying each other's burdens, one in working out our salvation, until the whole world is covered in the blood of Christ, praising God the Father, with the Holy Spirit "guiding" and "praying" alongside and through us. The church is holy because Christ is present in her, moving through her, kind of like the medieval idea of quintessence and ether moving through people's veins.

Now imagine for a moment what Christ's new blood covenant meant to medieval Christians, our kinsfolk in the kingdom, who understood the human body to contain four *humors* and *tempers*. The blood that coursed through their veins was full of *spiritus* ("breath," "life") or *animal* (*anima*, "soul") and was in constant relationship with the world around them, the atmosphere, the *ether* ("the upper air"), through which the celestial influences coursed. To participate in the blood covenant of God's only Son was to participate in the deepest, sweetest reality possible. It was to join in the song of the spheres, the ceaseless worship of Christ that holds the universe together. When we step back into their shoes, we begin to pick up the scent of a God-bathed world.

We could learn from these ancient believers. In a world where everything was surging and bubbling over with the Word of God, for the Christians of yore living the resurrection in their daily lives was a real possibility. Paul mused, "Some skeptic is sure to ask, 'Show me how resurrection works. Give me a diagram; draw me a picture. What does this "resurrection body" look like?' If you look at this question closely, you realize how absurd it is. There are no diagrams for this kind of thing" (1 Cor. 15:35–36 MSG). It is mostly because of the "intellectual pharisaism" of the modern era that we forget just how incarnational and eschatological the Lord's Table—indeed, the whole world—is.[6] We might ask with Nicodemus, "How can this be?" (John 3:9). But we must also pray, "Lord, I believe; help my unbelief!"

Part 7

Final
Participation

In Which our holy pilgrimage through enchanted Christianity comes to an end. Tyler and Britta visit Winston and Rose. The human heart is left of center. Christians are called to keep the neighborhood weird and wonderful, to be salt in a spoiling world. There is hope in the horror. We are participants in God's unfolding story of creation and redemption. We get to make preparations for a holy renaissance.

[The church] is the cosmos of the cosmos, because Christ has become its cosmos, he who is the primal light of the cosmos.

—Origen, *Commentary on the Gospel of John*

They will see his face, and his name will be on their foreheads. There will be no more night. They will not need the light of a lamp or the light of the sun, for the Lord God will give them light. And they will reign for ever and ever.

—Revelation 22:4–5

Chapter 26

Death by Water

Even after two millennia, it's still hard to believe that Jesus emerged from our world's humble backcountry, Nazareth. His plain but prophetic visage towers in icons—a gross and swarthy beard adorning a gaunt frame wrapped in itchy garments, warm but sunken eyes flashing in the Middle Eastern sun. He was a Jewish rabbi, a carpenter whose best friends were fishermen, an incredibly quotable vagabond preacher man who spoke with precision and absolute authority. His sentences are immortal:

> *"Do not judge, and you will not be judged" (Luke 6:37).*
> *"Give back to Caesar what is Caesar's, and to God what is God's" (Matt. 22:21).*
> *"The thief comes only to steal and kill and destroy; I have come that they may have life, and have it to the full" (John 10:10).*
> *"I am the way and the truth and the life. No one comes to the Father except through me" (John 14:6).*
> *"Seek first his kingdom and his righteousness, and all these things will be given to you as well" (Matt. 6:33).*
> *"What good is it for someone to gain the whole world, yet forfeit their soul?" (Mark 8.36).*

It was Jesus who coined the phrases "den of thieves," "signs of the times," "salt of the earth," and "pearls before swine," to name only a few. It is rare that one whose flame burned so brightly should burn so long. And I do not mean to speak flippantly of him. Jesus was no alien. Nor had he just dodged the psych wards. I try to imagine the tone of his voice as he spurned fans and baffled squares, proclaiming the arrival of the "kingdom of God." I believe there was not a dishonest bone in his body. I believe he is who he professed to be — the very Son of God, the promised Messiah, our Lord and Savior. This is one reason why Paul said the gospel is a "stumbling block." Very few of us want to hear we need a savior.

"They that are whole need not a physician; but they that are sick," Jesus boldly announced. "I came not to call the righteous, but sinners to repentance" (Luke 5:31 – 32 KJV). But who will admit that they are sick? Who will confess they are a horrible shipwrecked mess and need a savior? Only the honest, and only the brave. Only the uncool.

For a lot of us, our salvation stories are the story of our deaths. Tyler Blanski's coolness passed away without dignity when he was twelve years old. The location of his death was a kitschy church camp in the north woods of Wisconsin, where he lost a brave battle with lameness. Even at age twelve, he knew he just couldn't live for youthful good looks, rock-hard abs, the hunt for money, or the dream of great sex. Even then he knew he was what Jesus said he was: a horrible sinner made in the image of God in need of a savior who loves him. His friends tried everything to revive any amount of coolness Blanski had left, but it was way too late. Instead of accepting prestigious invitations to high school parties, Blanski's geekiness chose to stay home and read the Bible. Instead of setting his sights on a rock-star adolescence, he led worship at a megachurch. After numerous near-death experiences, Blanski's coolness finally underwent an emergency operation in the form of baptism at the age of fifteen. Growing up in a thoroughly unsacramental Baptist subculture, he was baptized on the shores of a suburban lake, holding hands with twenty other youths as they walked into a cold, wet lake for the great baptismal plunge. Funeral services for Blanski's coolness are held in an Anglican church in the Midwest every week, where his corpse can be found with all the other corpses. In lieu of flowers, his new family suggests the bread and wine of Holy Eucharist.

Jesus, the bearded and polarizing God-man around whom our calendars are dated, came preaching that we must die. He claimed we are all sinners, but sinners who are loved by God so much that he lay down his life for us. And in Baptism we are invited to die to our old cool selves—our worldliness and sinfulness—and to be raised up with Christ. The way the apostle Peter put it haunts me: "God waited patiently in the days of Noah while the ark was being built. In it only a few people, eight in all, were saved through water, and this water symbolizes baptism that now saves you also" (1 Peter 3:20–21). *Only eight persons were spared!* The well-known story of Noah's ark and the flood that buried the entire known world in a sea of green water is a horror story. While the rest of humanity climbed onto rooftops or shinnied up trees only to find with a last desperate gasp that the water would not stop rising, as the rest of humanity slowly drowned in the swirling flash flood, *a meager eight persons* were brought to safety. And Peter says *this* corresponds to Baptism?

Normally, when we talk about Baptism, we get the warm fuzzies. We tend to focus on how, in Baptism, we are raised up with Christ into new life. We like to focus on Peter's first baptismal reference in 1 Peter 1:3, "In [God's] great mercy he has given us new birth into a living hope through the resurrection of Jesus Christ from the dead" or 1 Peter 1:23, "You have been born again." But here Peter reminds us that there is a darker, even painful side to Baptism. You cannot be born anew unless you first die.

Some people scoff at Christianity. They think religion is a crutch, an emotional cushion for the timid and weak-minded. "Faith is an *easy out*," this line of reasoning goes. "Who wouldn't want the comfort of a loving God?" But Christianity is *not* safe. The gospel of Jesus Christ is anything but the high and easy road. You cannot have salvation without damnation. To accept Jesus as Lord and Savior is to accept a world where *all* have sinned and fallen short of the glory of God, all have gone astray, where each of us has warped and twisted the image of God impressed on us into a diseased, leprous narcissism. There is no one righteous, not even one. There is no one who understands. No one who seeks God. All have turned away. To believe what Jesus is saying is to believe that the whole sweep of human history apart from God has culminated in the twenty-first-century hipster: jaded, sarcastic, desperate for a teenage dream in the face of a yawning, cankerous vacuum. The fruit of sin is ripe and rotting. It produces nothing but isolation, fear, anger, the misuse of the earth and the abuse of other people, even ourselves. Is it any wonder that the revenue of sin is death?

We might like to think we are the exception to the rule but only because we conveniently ignore our abuse of oil, our exploitation of international labor, and our endorsement of something as monstrous as a megamall. We overlook what we do in dark rooms with a strong Internet connection and what we delight to watch on television. Even Christians are proud to flaunt their healthy bodies and their manicured lawns yet timid to flaunt righteousness and truth. If we are to take this wild and woolly God-man at his word, we are forced to admit that, like those in the days of Noah, we too deserve to die. Death. Death by water.

But there is hope in the horror. The flood is not the end of the story. Sin and death are not the last word. "For Christ also suffered once for sins, the righteous for the unrighteous, to bring you to God. He was put to death in the body but made alive in the Spirit" (1 Peter 3:18). We not only need to drown in the floodwaters; we need to be lifted up into a new life with Christ. This is the *gift* of Baptism: we get to die to our old sinful selves and to be reborn in the light and life of Christ's boundless love.

Baptism is a death sentence, a death by water, but it is also an invitation to a new life, a life washed and made clean in the blood of Jesus that was shed for us. By the blood of Christ's wounds we are — truly — *healed*. This washing, this deep cleaning, is so much more than cosmetic. The sacrament of Baptism is not exfoliation: Baptism is *regeneration*. It is a scouring of the heart, a deep scrubbing of the deepest part of your soul.[1]

For the early church, Baptism was the "key of the kingdom of heaven," the "water of life," the "garment of immortality," the "shining robe," the "chariot of God."[2] Cyril of Alexandria (376–444) held that perfect knowledge of Christ and complete participation in him are won only through the sacrament of Baptism and the corresponding illumination of the Holy Spirit.[3] According to Athanasius of Alexandria (296–373), it is through the sacred waters of Baptism that we are united with the Godhead, and it is through this sacrament of regeneration that the divine image is renewed.[4]

But here's the rub: we will never step into the divine inheritance if we do not die a death by water.[5] In chapter 1, Peter recalls how some of the Israelites who passed through the baptismal waters of the Red Sea, from slavery into freedom, tragically yearned to return to the luxurious and hedonistic living of Egypt. They had no taste for the things of God. We have to get wet. We have to take the plunge, and we can't look back. To enter the Promised Land, we must leave Egypt behind. To enter the kingdom of God, we must allow our love of this world to drown in tidal floods as in the days of Noah. To truly live our Baptism, we must die to our old selves and be lifted up in Christ. There can be no rival love. Only Christ can remain.

This is what I'm trying to do with my crazy-ass theory, my exploring the old-time days of Christendom: I'm trying to have Christ be my presupposition, the one thing I take as a given, my only premise. I'm attempting to learn how to renew my mind so that I might see the whole world in the light of Jesus. I want the law of God, his holy covenants, to be more real for me than the law of gravity.

When we were baptized, what were we baptized into if not a covenant with Jesus Christ? In Genesis 9:8 – 17 we read that Noah and his family passed *through* the baptismal waters of the flood *and into* a holy covenant, a covenant sealed with the sign of a rainbow. In only a few verses, the word covenant shows up seven times; and for the Israelites, seven was a sacred number. A covenant is a sacred God-initiated and God-sustained relationship with his people. God's covenants are more real than anything else on earth. Who are we to fathom the weight, the gravitas, of God's holy covenants? God preordained his covenant with man before the world was made. The baptismal covenant is truer and more reliable than the law of gravity. Covenants are a deep magic. They run deeper than the dawn of time. Not even the devil can fathom the depth and breadth of God's sacred covenants.

Baptism marks our death. But it also signifies our new and vibrant life in the one triune God who is lord over all things in heaven and in hell and on earth and for eternity!

I try to wrap my mind around it. When Jesus was baptized in water, the Holy Spirit descended on him like a dove. Similarly, when Noah was in the ark, he released a dove to rove over the waters. And from the beginning, even from Genesis 1, we read that the "Spirit of God was hovering over the waters" (v. 2). Doves and water and wind and fluttering and the Spirit of the living God. God is incredibly close, closer than ever. The kingdom of God is actually at our doorsteps! It is extremely and perilously nigh!

But will we live out our baptisms? Will we put away our old selves and put on Jesus? Will we embrace the death sentence, death by water?

> *Jesus [said to Nicodemus], "Very truly I tell you, no one can see the kingdom of God unless they are born again."*
>
> *"How can someone be born when they are old?" Nicodemus asked. "Surely they cannot enter a second time into their mother's womb to be born!"*
>
> *Jesus answered, "Very truly I tell you, no one can enter the kingdom of God unless they are born of water and the Spirit. Flesh gives birth to flesh, but the Spirit gives birth to spirit. You should not be surprised at my saying, 'You must be born again.' The wind blows wherever it pleases. You hear its sound, but you cannot tell where it comes from or where it is going. So it is with everyone born of the Spirit."*
>
> *"How can this be?" Nicodemus asked. (John 3:3–9)*

And who can help but wonder with him: How *can* these things be?

Chapter 27

The New Community

If I had a list, dinner at Rose and Winston's would be among my top five favorite things to do. It's more than the huge Great Danes, the good southern grub, and their joyful children who smell like apple juice and fill their home with laughter. Just being around them is edifying because they are so wise and loving.

I was nearing the end of my holy pilgrimage when Rose and Winston invited me over again, this time with Britta. She was wearing a fashionable shawl from Italy; I was sporting my favorite flannel. After a game of Scrabble, we moved from the kitchen table to the living room. The kids sounded like they were waging war with Lord Voldemort in what Winston calls the rumpus room. I thought Rose moved regally for being pregnant, like a southern belle, as she eased into a rocking chair and rubbed her sizable stomach. A roast was slow-cooking in the Crock-Pot, and Winston went to check it and put another pot of coffee on.

"How do you like it?" Rose asked.

"Same as ever. Black."

"I mean, how do you feel about your book so far?" she asked with a tinkle of laughter.

"Aha," I said, wrinkling my brow. "To be honest, I feel like I'm in way over my head."

"In what way?" asked Britta, curled up in the corner of a couch with an empty coffee mug.

"Here I am writing about talking donkeys and deep magic and covenants that sweep us up into the story of God, and then I go to church and the actual faces in my pew just don't seem as epic as what the Bible describes. Bad breath, singing out of tune, weirdos and Waldos—sometimes it's hard to see how church is the new community the Bible talks about."

"Strange, coming from the dork with the medieval beard and motorcycle boots," Britta said, looking at me with surprise. "What do you expect Christians to look like? Knights in shining armor and monks in russet robes?"

I was instantly embarrassed. She was right, of course. Jesus has always filled his church with ordinary people, just like me. "It's just hard to believe that the whole world is groaning under the strain of our slowly becoming remade and whole in Christ, waiting for us to grow into our destined role to rule the universe, into 'the coming glory to be revealed in us.'"

Rose stood up from her rocking chair and went to get her old, worn American Standard Version. "You know, Ty, it's always baffled me that God is literally dwelling in ordinary folks like us. To Jacob's youngest son, the cupcake in a colorful robe, God gives the gifts of dreams and interpretation. Joseph goes from being a slave and prisoner to a prince with great power. To the little boy David, who was overlooked by his own father, Jesse, God gives the strength to slay Goliath. This shepherd becomes the noble king of Israel. From the young Samuel, to the outback hillbillies Elijah and Elisha, God works with the tiny and the overlooked to get stuff done. It's what I like to call *irony*."

She gave me a philosophical look. "The Lord makes a home with us in just the strangest ways," she continued. "I mean, God chose to inhabit a tent — of all things, a *tent!* — for years of desert camping," she said, somehow fitting three syllables into the word *tent*. She flipped through the Old Testament to Exodus: "And I will sanctify the tent of meeting, and the altar: Aaron also and his sons will I sanctify, to minister to me in the priest's office. And I will dwell among the children of Israel, and will be their God. And they shall know that I am Jehovah their God, that brought them forth out of the land of Egypt, that I might dwell among them: I am Jehovah their God" (29:44–47 ASV).

Winston sauntered back into the room, proudly sporting an apron with a huge lobster on it and a carafe of hot coffee. Britta and I held out our mugs, and he filled them with the rich, aromatic brew.

"It's like shoving your face in a bouquet of mixed nuts and cacao beans, ain't it?" he asked her. He had a strange way of talking about coffee as if it were fine wine.

"Um-hm." Britta smiled. "Couldn't be better!"

"Is it decaf?" asked Rose, eyeing the carafe with concern. Winston loved coffee almost as much as he loved wine and was having a hard time adjusting to his wife's newfound love of decaf.

"I'm sorry, darling," he said, looking very guilty.

"I love you to pieces, mister," she said, and kissed his cheek.

"I love you to pieces back," he said, quickly cheering.

"Tea would be lovely dear."

"Yes, ma'am," Winston said with a grin, and marched to the kitchen with purpose and his strange apron, stepping over the two Great Danes who had flopped down in the doorway. Rose sat back down.

"The way I see it," continued Rose, "the way God indwelled that tent is like the way he indwells the church today. You can't read Ephesians without picking up clues that God is making a redeemed community out of ordinary people like you and me. Soon the church will spread through the entire world and join God in governing it."

"I wonder why?" asked Britta, cupping her mug in both hands.

"Because, through Christians," said Rose with conviction, "God's love can be known. Church is where it all starts."

Sunlight splashed into the room. Rose turned to Ephesians, the Bible resting on her belly, and read: "So then ye are no more strangers and sojourners, but ye are fellow-citizens with the saints, and of the household of God, being built upon the foundation of the apostles and prophets, Christ Jesus himself being the chief corner stone; in whom each several building, fitly framed together, groweth into a holy temple in the Lord; in whom ye also are builded together for a habitation of God in the Spirit" (2:19 – 22).

She closed the Bible. "You see," she said, her cheeks flushed, "after so much preparation, Jesus brought salvation, 'to make all men see what is the dispensation of the mystery which for ages hath been hid in God who created all things,'" she quoted from Ephesians (3:9).

Winston came back in jiggling and burping their youngest baby girl. He handed Rose her tea and with his free arm poured himself a glass of wine. I was amazed by his dexterity. With dinner approaching, no one was surprised to see this sommelier had moved on to Pinot Noir.

"I think it's so beautiful," Britta said, her eyes bright. "God's way of making his covenants known is to transform human hearts by living with them, one person at a time. He finds an Abraham, a Moses, a David, a Paul, a Winston, or a Rose, and then slowly works out his plan for all humankind, and beyond."

Rose reached over and gently rested her palm on the baby's head. "It's so simple, so ordinary, yet so overwhelming a responsibility," she said. "A *glory*, really."

" 'For our light and momentary troubles are achieving for us an eternal glory that far outweighs them all,' " Winston said with fervor (2 Cor. 4:17). We all watched the fading sunlight warm the wood floor. A loud thud could be heard from the rumpus room, followed by heavy sobs. My coffee had gone cold. The Crock-Pot was making strange noises. Soon no one was thinking about glory.

Feeling strangely moved, I went to the kitchen and refilled my coffee mug. I shook my head, trying to clear it. They were all spot on. The fruit of Baptism is not simply a better, more moral, or happier life, but a life *ontologically* different from the old one. This difference, this "new life" that Paul talks about, is *life with Christ*. "If we died with Christ, we believe that we will also live with him" (Rom. 6:8). Just because someone thinks they're a Christian, doesn't make them one. It is *Jesus'* risen life that is given to us, *his* resurrection life that becomes our resurrection life. "Don't you know that all of us who were baptized into Christ Jesus were baptized into his death?" Paul asked. "We were therefore buried with him through baptism into death in order that, just as Christ was raised from the dead through the glory of the Father, we too may live a new life" (Rom. 6:3–4). And this newness of life is found only in the church, which is Christ in us together, his coming presence, the sacrament of his sharing his resurrection life with us. "Behold!" Joshua the Messiah reminds us. "I am *with* you always, to the very end of the age" (Matt. 28:20, italics mine).

Because of Jesus, all of us ragtag and slipshod folks can go to church like we actually own the place. Jesus is the pioneer of the resurrection life. He opens the way for others to follow. "See, I will create new heavens and a new earth" (Isa. 65:17; cf. 2 Peter 3:13; Rev. 21:1–4). That afternoon at Winston's, I realized what a humbling thing it is that God would use ragamuffins like you and me to do it.

Chapter 28

Reorienting Our Loves

People often ask if "Jesus is God" — as if the "God" part is known and the "Jesus" part is unknown. But it's the other way around.[1] In an effort to be "neutral" or "objective," it is widely assumed that "God" is actually "God's" actual name, and that any worship of any god by monotheists and polytheists alike is wonderfully decoded into worship of one "God." Even though Judaism, Christianity, and Islam (all monotheist religions) ardently believe this concept to be self-evidently untrue, and even though Hinduism and Buddhism (and other polytheist religions) also believe this to be self-evidently untrue, the contemporary "neutral" and "objective" assumption is that all of the major religions are basically worshiping the same "God." Thus the contemporary assumption is that if any one of these religions claimed to have the truth about "God," it would be dismissed as ignorant, dogmatic, and even arrogant. To postmodern pluralists, then, the question of whether "Jesus is God" is a perfectly legitimate one, because they think they have God figured out.

How postmodern pluralists manage to look down from some great and "neutral" Olympian height and accuse all the major religions of the world of playing religious games is a mystery to me. "There is an admirable air of humility about the statement that the truth is much greater than any one person or any one religious tradition can grasp," observed Lesslie Newbigin. But he went on to ask, "How does the speaker know that the truth is so much greater than this particular affirmation of it—for example, that 'Jesus Christ is the truth'? What privileged access to reality does he have?"[2] The honest answer is, he has no exceptional access to truth. His claim that Jesus and Allah are little more than different translations of the same divine language is mere speculation, a naive truth claim with no facts and no warrant. He does not work from a surplus of data but from a paucity of data. He has merely assumed that *his* idea of an ultimately indefinable and unknowable God who apparently reveals himself in contradictory ways is *the* ultimate reality.

Jesus, the Word who became flesh and dwelt among us, is what we know about God. "God" is not a benign unknown deity. His name is Joshua the Anointed One, Jesus the Messiah, the second person of the Holy Trinity. God is known specifically as the Father, the Son, and the Holy Spirit. And when Christians are baptized, we are baptized into the living body of Jesus, his one catholic and holy and apostolic church, not a private one-on-one interview. God is known through Jesus Christ, and Jesus Christ is known through the Holy Spirit, and ever since Pentecost the Holy Spirit has been active in the church. This is why at Baptism and the Lord's Supper, the eclectic and ecumenical congregation of believers is participating in Christ's divinity. Just as the sky was torn open at Jesus' baptism and the Holy Spirit descended on him like a dove, the temple curtain has been torn apart and a new day of God's reign on earth has begun.[3]

I want to dust off our telescopes, to behold again that the heavens are telling of the glory of God, to marvel at "the sacred canopy," to appropriate a phrase from Peter Berger. This tapestry has been torn. It has been privatized and relativized. But I believe this sacred canopy, stretching from Genesis to Revelation, is public knowledge and objective truth. God is reigning. His kingdom *is* reality. The gospel of Jesus Christ is our *only* reigning plausibility structure. Standing between Christ's ascension and his final restoration of all things, we are called to be a mission outpost of God's reign, to join Christ in his renewal project. The church is not a place to buy religious goods to bring into our private life; it is the outward visible sign of Christ, a corporate sacrament of Jesus.

To live in the body of Christ in the present tense, we need to know where we have been and what our future is going to be like. In some senses, we must become medieval. By "become medieval" I not only mean that we must allow the Christocentric intellectual and spiritual vision of the Middle Age to deepen our faith today but that we must restore a sense of living in a Middle Age ourselves.

Augustine spoke of living "in this age that comes in the middle (*in hoc interim saeculo*)."[4] By this he meant that we are in a middle era where the City of God and the City of Man are intermingled until the last judgment. In the seventh century, Julian of Toledo spoke of "a middle age (*tempus medium*)" that came "between the two comings of Christ, the first in the incarnation, and the second in judgment."[5] So says the apostle John: "See what great love the Father has lavished on us, that we should be called children of God! And that is what we are! The reason the world does not know us is that it did not know him. Dear friends, now we are children of God, and what we will be has not yet been made known. But we know that when Christ appears, we shall be like him, for we shall see him as he is" (1 John 3:1–2). The kingdom of God is here already—though not yet fulfilled. This "already–not yet" state is our Middle Age. Though Jesus has conquered sin and death once and for all, salvation must still be realized more fully in the unfolding history of his body, the church.

We are called to keep the neighborhood weird and wonderful, to be salt in a spoiling world. We are called to know our dough, to be filled with the yeast of the Holy Spirit. The exalted Christ poured out his Spirit on his church, and the Spirit formed a new community, a *koinonia* (Acts 2:14–47; 6:7; 12:24; 19:20). Jesus told his followers to wait in Jerusalem and promised that the Holy Spirit would be poured out on them (Luke 24:49; Acts 1:4–5; 2:37–47). And indeed, the Holy Spirit came in power on the Jewish Feast of Pentecost, the feast when Israel brought the firstfruits of the harvest to God in anticipation of the whole crop that would later be gathered in (Ex. 23:16; Deut. 16:9–12). That day when a violent wind suddenly filled the house and tongues of fire came to rest on the disciples' heads signified the firstfruits of the coming kingdom of God, now open to the whole world. The loving and sharing new community, the Spirit-filled body of Christ, radiates the light of the new covenant and draws people out from the darkness. Beginning with the original disciples and on throughout all of church history, "day after day, in the temple courts and from house to house," Christians have "never stopped teaching and proclaiming the good news that Jesus is the Messiah" (Acts 5:42). Even Midwest folks like Winston and Rose and Britta can join them.

When we were born again, the salvific work of Christ the God-man became our work. Yet many of us, alas, have suffered the malpractice of pastors who dilute Scripture into the language of media and pop culture, repackage the gospel into materialistic or therapeutic deism, or simply turn the poetry of Christ into drudgery. In some circles, *discipleship* has become a dirty word. It's another word for legalism. But being moralistic is not what Jesus means when he calls us to discipleship. The word *Christian* appears only three times in the New Testament. The word *disciple*, or *student*, appears nearly three hundred times. To be a disciple (*discipulus*, "learner") is to be a student. Before Christ-followers are Christians, they are first disciples enrolled in the master class of life, the kingdom life. Christendom is not a museum of saints, but a hospital for sinners, a school for the broken.

Before it is anything else, discipleship is a *reorienting of our loves*. There is no legalistic checklist in this class: only the invitation to become lifelong, wholehearted lovers of God the Father, Son, and Holy Spirit. At first this reorientation can feel like disorientation. We lived upside down and inside out so long in our sin that we thought it was normal. But being a student of Christ turns everything right side up. It invites us to saddle our proverbial donkeys and hobble out of the mists of modern idolatry and into the light of Christ.

The idolatry of Atomland says, "Because I think, therefore I exist." It says this because godlessness naturally leads to nihilism, narcissism, and inflated self-love. In Atomland, *I* come first; *I* decide what is truth. Students in the kingdom of God, however, say, "I am because God is. I love because he loves me. Because I love, I think; and because I am sinful, sometimes I think idolatrous thoughts like, 'I think, therefore I am,' as if I were God." When we live in the love of God, allowing Jesus to renew our hearts and minds, our loves are reoriented. We are no longer the harbingers of truth. We live in the trail of God's salvation stories, of his love. When we apprentice ourselves to Jesus, we are enrolling in a class of love.

"If anyone comes to me and does not hate father and mother, wife and children, brothers and sisters — yes, even their own life — such a person cannot be my disciple" (Luke 14:26). To think Jesus is here saying we should literally hate those we love would be to read this passage outside of the context of his whole life of love and his death on the cross. Jesus is saying that if we want to be his disciples, his students, we must *reorder our loves*. We must love Joshua the Christ, the Promised One, before all else. I think some pastors misinterpret this reordering of loves to mean that we should be "more balanced" in how we love others. The idea is we love our wives and children, fathers and mothers, too much. But can any of us honestly say we do not love God because we love our neighbors too much? The notion is grossly self-flattering. If anything, we do not love our brothers and sisters enough. The heart is not balanced in the middle of your chest. It's just to the left, off center. The human heart defies balance. Our problem is not that we love our friends and families too much but that we do not love them enough. We do not love them enough because we do not love God enough.

When Jesus says we must "hate" our parents and spouses and children, he is saying that the heart *cannot* be balanced. It can't be compartmentalized. We cannot divide up our loves and give the remainder to God. It's all or nothing. We must love God with our whole hearts. God's love is an inexhaustible resource. When we love God with our whole bodies, our whole hearts, our whole minds, until we are completely consumed with love for him, we won't have to worry about not having enough love for our children or neighbors. We will love them more. When we are undivided, all in, and totally in love with our Lord, the whole world becomes all the more lovable. But God must come first. He alone is the Holy One, he alone is the Lord, he alone is the Most High, Jesus Christ, with the Holy Spirit, in the glory of God the Father.[6]

Chapter 29

Come, Have Breakfast

I love reading the accounts of the crucified and resurrected Jesus appearing to his apostles. It is such an emotional time. They are still grieving their crucified Lord, yet all is green and springtime new, and they don't even know it yet. And then Christ comes to them, and in the strangest, most beautiful ways. In all of the stories of where the risen Jesus meets with his apprentices, Jesus is physically present; to erase the apostles' doubt, he invites them to touch him, to touch his wounds, and he even eats with them. He tells them about their new mission.

In the gospel of Luke, we get a beautiful snapshot of life with the resurrected Christ. Two disciples were walking down a winding road that led to Emmaus, their minds and hearts caught in a whirlwind of confusion and emotion. The death-conquering Jesus "came up and walked along with them; but they were kept from recognizing him" (Luke 24:15 – 16). He explained the Scriptures to them, recounting how he fulfilled the law and was bringing about a restoration of all things, and they invited him to eat with them. That night, when Jesus blessed bread and broke it, "their eyes were opened and they recognized him" (v. 31). And they said to one another, "Were not our hearts burning within us while he talked with us on the road and opened the Scriptures to us?" (v. 32).

What is striking about this beautiful story is that in the breaking of the bread the apostles recognized Christ. I am reminded of the account of Mary Magdalene in the garden on the morning of Jesus' resurrection. The story highlights not only that Jesus was present but that he was *recognized*. The resurrected Messiah is identified and known in the plain gesture of breaking bread or in a single word, "Mary."

As a traveler on holy pilgrimage, constantly eating trinitarian breakfasts and reading stories about the magical and miraculous, I love that at the end of John we also see Jesus meeting the apostles for breakfast. After Jesus miraculously fills their nets with fish, he lights a charcoal fire and lays the fish on it, and bread, and says to them, "Come and have breakfast." At that moment, they recognize him as the Lord (John 21:1 – 14). Again, it is in the breaking of the bread that the resurrection becomes a tangible and recognizable reality. Jesus did not only appear to the disciples: there on the shore of the sea in the early morning light, he broke bread with them, and when they ate they suddenly *recognized* his lordship.

This recognition of God, this remarkable encounter with the divine in the eating of bread, was carried on as a tradition among the apostles. This tradition reminded them of and re-membered them into a covenant between God and his people that filled empty nets with fish, healed the blind with mud, and was made known to the lowly. To the apostolic church, this *participation* in God at the Holy Eucharist was, in the richest sense of the word, a mystery (μυστηριον, *mysterion*). It is the mark of future hope: "I tell you," promised Christ, "I will not drink of this fruit of the vine from now on until that day when I drink it new with you in my Father's kingdom" (Matt. 26:29) — in other words, until that day when the covenantal restoration of all things comes to completion.

Chapter 30

A Holy Renaissance

A holy renaissance — that is my prayer. Together becoming students of Jesus. Going back to the sources. Being fed by passages of Scripture. Entering the long and curious story of God-on-earth, the tradition. Chewing on the wisdom of those who have gone before us, the saints. Being nourished by the sacraments. Daily practicing and nurturing God's salvation with that involuntary shaking and reverent fear Paul talks about (Phil. 2:12). And most of all, getting out of the way — or becoming a way — for God to heal and love broken people, to join the Holy Trinity in making even more salvation stories.

I am not asking you to be so benighted as to believe in pixies. But I am asking that you become foolish enough to become a fool for Christ. Let us rediscover the reign of God in reality. Let us recover a sense of living in a world held together by more than gravity and laws, a cosmos held together by the covenants of God and his people, a world that sings of God's glory, a world where even donkeys can talk. It's a reclamation project, an effort to become more closely grafted to "the vine" of Christ. We can follow God's lead to prepare a new community of prayer and collective obedience to God, churches rooted in Word and sacrament, divine revelation and tradition, and the abundant life found in Jesus. For God has set it up in such a way that the fulfillment of his kingdom might be made known "through the church" (Eph. 3:10). We are his co-creators, accomplices in this cosmic project of renewal.

Christianity does not have to be fashion-bound to the American religious experiments of the twentieth century. It does not have to try to host a dance party in the tiny cubicle of modernity. For me, hobbling around on an imaginary donkey has been one way to step out of the hype of a heavily marketed and carefully catered American God. Christianity has always been so much more than a megamall shopping experience or a self-help book. It's the best way of life possible—a God-infused life of community, creation care, and genuinely lived love. As disciples of Jesus, we are part of the ongoing salvation narrative of the Jesus who entered real history and changes real lives. A renaissance, by definition, invites us into that story. It is ancient, but it is also timeless.

I hope that praying for a holy renaissance does not reduce the sovereign work of God into little more than a human reform agenda. It is quite the other way around. A holy renaissance will happen only when we discard our reform agendas and surrender ourselves to the sovereign activity of God. Only when we pick up the rhythms of the kingdom of God will we see a holy renaissance.

Reading the Bible, I find it difficult to define the kingdom of God as a single empirical state of affairs or "thing." It has come near, it has come upon us, we can enter it, it is in the midst of us, it is taken by force, it suffers violence, it has been prepared and is being prepared, it has keys and can be locked, we can be great or least in it, and we pray for it in the Lord's Prayer. In biblical context, the kingdom of God is already present and yet to come. It is an eternal reality *and* a future hope. It has been inaugurated in Christ but has not yet been fulfilled, is yet to be consummated. The kingdom is the context of God's sovereign purpose. It impinges on all of life, and it was the heart of Jesus' whole mission. It is *his* initiative, *his* purpose accomplished, *his* reign—and it is what the whole world is about.[1]

Today we get to make plans for a holy renaissance, to live in trust of what God promises us when we practice disciplines of discipleship to Jesus and open ourselves up to the Holy Spirit: real love, abiding joy, patience, genuine kindness, true generosity, trusting faithfulness, gentleness, and voluntary self-control (cf. Gal. 5). We get to savor and digest the living Word of God and to receive the sacraments of Baptism and the Lord's Supper. We get to step into the ongoing story of salvation we call the tradition, to live the faith and pray the prayers of the students of Jesus' way who have gone before us. And, as humbling as it is to face directly, God has given us the task of bringing about his kingdom.

As far as I can tell—and I am, after all, only on a donkey—the kingdom of God is extremely nigh. Holy water is everywhere. We need only to bless it. We live as creatures in creation, as participants in a blood-covenanted world. There is nary a hair on your head that will go unaccounted, not a corner of this world that will escape Baptism. The kingdom of God is seriously nigh. We are on the brink. No, we are already swimming.

Epilogue

The Song of Isaiah

"See, I will create
new heavens and a new earth.
The former things will not be remembered,
nor will they come to mind.
But be glad and rejoice forever
in what I will create,
for I will create Jerusalem to be a delight
and its people a joy.
I will rejoice over Jerusalem
and take delight in my people;
the sound of weeping and of crying
will be heard in it no more.

"Never again will there be in it
an infant who lives but a few days,
or an old man who does not live out his years;
the one who dies at a hundred
will be thought a mere child;
the one who fails to reach a hundred
will be considered accursed.
They will build houses and dwell in them;

they will plant vineyards and eat their fruit.
No longer will they build houses and others live in them,
    or plant and others eat.
For as the days of a tree,
    so will be the days of my people;
my chosen ones will long enjoy
    the work of their hands.
They will not labor in vain,
    nor will they bear children doomed to misfortune;
For they will be a people blessed by the LORD,
    they and their descendants with them.
Before they call I will answer;
    while they are still speaking I will hear.
The wolf and the lamb will feed together,
    and the lion will eat straw like the ox,
    and dust will be the serpent's food.
They will neither harm nor destroy
    on all my holy mountain,"
    says the LORD.

Isaiah 65:17–25

Notes

Chapter 1 - Holy Pilgrimage

1. "I wouldn't be able to defy the orders of my GOD to do anything" (Num. 22:18 MSG). Martin Noth comments, "(Balaam), as the recipient of revelation, was aware that Yahweh ruled the whole of world history, even although he himself was not part of the 'people of Yahweh.'" Martin Noth, *Numbers: A Commentary*, Old Testament Library (Philadelphia: Westminster John Knox, 1969), 174.

2. Cf. Talmud, *Berakot* 7a; Num. 22:6, 8, 20, 35, 38; 23:4, 18; 24:3, 15–24.

3. Walter Riggans, *Numbers*, Old Testament Daily Study Bible Series (Philadelphia: Westminster John Knox, 1983), 164.

4. Ibid.

5. Cf. Gordon J. Wenham, *Numbers: An Introduction and Commentary*, Tyndale Old Testament Commentaries (Downers Grove, IL: InterVarsity, 1981), 164.

6. "[This passage] is in fact making the point that the medium of God's message is not important—only the message is. An ass or an angel, it doesn't matter." Riggans, *Numbers*, 170.

7. *Weird* means "suggesting something supernatural or uncanny," as in "the weird crying of an ass." King Alfred the Great once said, "What we call Wyrd is really the work of God about which He is busy every day." From Alfred's translation of Boethius: quoted in Brian Branson, *The Lost Gods of England* (New York: Thames & Hudson, 1957), 59.

8. Saint Cyprian, *The Lapsed/The Unity of the Catholic Church*, trans. Maurice Bevenot (Long Prairie, MN: Neumann, 1956), 13.

9. Ambrose Autpert, *Commentary on the Apocalypse*, 1. Cf. Jaroslav Pelikan, *The Growth of Medieval Theology* (Chicago: Univ. of Chicago Press, 1978), 43.

10. Cf. C. S. Lewis, *The Discarded Image* (Cambridge: Cambridge Univ. Press, 1974); Owen Barfield, *History in English Words* (London: Faber & Faber, 1953), 169.

Chapter 2 - In Search of Magic

1. Apuleius, *The Metamorphoses*, trans. Robert Grave (New York: Farrar, Straus & Giroux, 1979), 71.

2. Miguel de Cervantes, *Don Quixote*, trans. John Rutherford (New York: Penguin, 2000), 119.

Chapter 3 - A Deepening Conversion

1. The term "moralistic therapeutic deism" is introduced in the book *Soul Searching: The Religious and Spiritual Lives of American Teenagers* by Christian Smith and Melinda Lundquist Denton (New York: Oxford Univ. Press, 2009).

Chapter 4 - A Restoration Project

1. Nicene Creed.

2. Justin Martyr, *Dialogue with Trypho* 8.2.

Chapter 5 - Taking the Donkey to the Dentist

1. This conversation is appropriated from G. K. Chesterton, *Orthodoxy* (London: Hodder and Stoughton, 1999), 87–95; C. S. Lewis, "Religion and Science," in *God in the Dock*, ed. Walter Hooper (Grand Rapids: Eerdmans, 1970), 72; Edward O. Wilson, *Consilience: The Unity of Knowledge* (New York: Vintage, 1998), 51; and Edward O. Wilson, *On Human Nature* (Cambridge: Harvard Univ. Press, 1978), 6–7.

2. Sam Harris, *The End of Faith: Religion, Terror, and the Future of Reason* (New York: W. W. Norton, 2004), 73.

Chapter 6 - Christendom and Atomland

1. Richard Dawkins, *A Devil's Chaplain: Reflections on Hope, Lies, Science, and Love* (New York: Houghton Mifflin, 2003), 143.

2. It is helpful to remember that our word *mechanic* comes from the Greek μηξηανη (*mexeane*), a "device" or "contrivance."

3. G. K. Chesterton, *Saint Thomas Aquinas* (New York: Image, 1956), 4.

4. As professor of medicine Sherwin Nuland likes to refer to it.

5. Erwin Chargaff, *Heraclitean Fire* (New York: Rockefeller Univ. Press, 1978), 170.

Chapter 7 - Saving the Appearances

1. "It is difficult to imagine a set of beliefs more suggestive of mental illness than those that lie at the heart of many of our religious traditions.... Theology is now little more than a branch of human ignorance. Indeed, it is ignorance with wings." Sam Harris, *The End of Faith: Religion, Terror, and the Future of Reason* (New York: W. W. Norton, 2004), 72, 173.

2. Ian Sample, "There Is No Heaven: It's a Fairy Story," guardian.co.uk, 18 May 2011.

3. Richard Dawkins, *River Out of Eden: A Darwinian View of Life* (New York: Basic, 1995), 18 – 19.

4. Edward O. Wilson, *On Human Nature* (Cambridge: Harvard Univ. Press, 1978), 54.

5. Edward O. Wilson, *Consilience: The Unity of Knowledge* (New York: Vintage, 1998), 33, 105.

6. Cf. Wilson, *On Human Nature*, 1 – 6. Wilson says elsewhere, "You say that science cannot explain spiritual phenomena. Why not? The brain sciences are making important advances in the analysis of the complex operations of the mind. There is no apparent reason why they cannot in time provide a material account of the emotions and ratiocination that compose spiritual thought." *Consilience*, 269. This is not an argument. This is deductive and circular reasoning of the worst sort.

7. Wilson, *Consilience*, 286. He earlier announces that evolution is "the most important revelation of all," and that since the Bible fails to mention evolution, the prophets could not "really have been privy to the thoughts of God" (6).

8. Ibid., 286.

9. Wilson, *On Human Nature*, 71.

10. "Confidence in free will is biologically adaptive" (Wilson, *Consilience*, 131); thus religion exists "to confer a biological advantage" (Wilson, *On Human Nature*, 188). "Religion itself is subject to the explanations of the natural sciences.... Sociobiology can account for the very origin of mythology by the principle of natural selection acting on the genetically

evolving material structure of the human brain.... The evolutionary epic is probably the best myth we will ever have." *On Human Nature*, 192, 201.

11. *Consilience*, 271. Interestingly, for centuries the biological meaning of *species* was only one of many. The word was once used by Cicero to translate Plato's "Idea." In medieval logic it was one of the five "predicables" by which an object could be defined. But since Darwin's *Origin of the Species* the coterie jargon of biologists who talk of people as if they were a *species* has become the unquestioned parlance of pop culture.

12. Wendell Berry, *Life Is a Miracle: An Essay against Modern Superstition* (Berkeley, CA: Counterpoint 2001), 29.

13. Simplicius, a sixth-century medieval thinker, coined this phrase in his commentary on Aristotle's *De Caelo*. To the ancient Greeks, *phainomenon* meant "a thing appearing to view." The word was used this way in Aristotle's *De Caelo*, a book that had enormous influence on antiquity and medieval Europe.

14. But again, as Owen Barfield says, "A representation, which is collectively mistaken for an ultimate — ought not to be called a representation. It is an idol. Thus the phenomena themselves are idols, when they are imagined as enjoying that independence of human perception which can in fact only pertain to the unrepresented." Owen Barfield, *Saving the Appearances: A Study in Idolatry* (London: Faber & Faber, 1988), 62.

15. "The human mind evolved to believe in the gods. It did not evolve to believe in biology." Wilson, *Consilience*, 286.

16. "The species lacks any goal external to its own biological nature.... Biology is the key to human nature." Wilson, *On Human Nature*, 3, 13.

17. Barfield, *Saving the Appearances*, 39. He says later, "Phenomena are experienced collectively *as* representations, and not as idols, where there is a survival of participation" (75).

18. The "two worlds" of Atomland and Christendom deliberately echo Augustine's *The City of God*. Although there are similarities, I do not mean them to reflect what the British scientist C. P. Snow calls "the two cultures," although his thesis illustrates the breakdown of communication between the sciences and the humanities.

19. "Those who think they know something do not yet know as they ought to know. But whoever loves God is known by God" (1 Cor. 8:2–3).

Chapter 8 - No One Is Listening

1. Edward O. Wilson, *Consilience: The Unity of Knowledge* (New York: Vintage, 1998), 271.

2. "The central idea of the consilience worldview is that all tangible phenomena," writes Wilson, "from the birth of stars to the workings of social institutions, are based on material processes that are ultimately reducible, however long and tortuous the sequences, to the laws of physics." Wilson, *Consilience*, 291. He says elsewhere that "(science's) strong form is total consilience, which holds that nature is organized by simple universal laws of physics to which all other laws and principles can eventually be reduced" (60).

3. "Our meddling intellect / Mis-shapes the beauteous forms of things:— / We murder to dissect." William Wordsworth, "The Tables Turned," in *Selected Poems and Prefaces*, ed. Jack Stillinger (Boston: Houghton Mifflin, 1965).

4. Erwin Chargaff writes on this "yet," poignantly: "The Nazi experiment in eugenics— 'the elimination of racially inferior elements'— was the outgrowth of the same kind of mechanistic thinking that, in an outwardly very different form, contributed to what most people would consider the glories of modern science. The diabolical dialectics of progress change causes into symptoms, symptoms into causes; the distinction between torturer and victim becomes merely a function of the plane of vision. Humanity has not learned—if I were a true scientist, i.e., an optimist, I should insert here the adverb 'yet'—how to call a halt to this dizzying tumble into the geometrical progression of disasters which we call progress." Erwin Chargaff, *Heraclitean Fire* (New York: Rockefeller Univ. Press, 1978), 5.

5. Wilson, *Consilience*, 11. When Wilson writes, "It is worth asking, particularly in the winter of our cultural discontent, whether the original spirit of the Enlightenment—confidence, optimism, eyes to the horizon—can be regained" (22), he is mimicking Shakespeare's Richard III, who also favored reductionism to no one's benefit; not even, in the end, his own (cf. William Shakespeare, *Richard III*, act 1, scene 1).

6. Bonaventure, *On the Threefold Way*, pr.1: quoted in Jaroslav Pelikan, *The Growth of Medieval Theology* (Chicago: Univ. of Chicago Press, 1978), 282.

Chapter 9 - Breakfast at the Modern

1. Cf. Bonaventure's *The Soul's Journey into God,* Classics of Western Spirituality Series (Mahwah, NJ: Paulist Press, 1978), and Bonhoeffer's *Christ the Center* (New York: Harper & Row, 1960). See also Rev. 22:13 and 1 Cor. 15:28.

2. "We are fools for Christ's sake, but you are wise in Christ. We are weak, but you are strong. You are held in honor, but we in disrepute. To the present hour we hunger and thirst, we are poorly dressed and buffeted and homeless, and we labor, working with our own hands. When reviled, we bless; when persecuted, we endure; when slandered, we entreat. We have become, and are still, like the scum of the world, the refuse of all things" (1 Cor. 4:10–13).

3. C. S. Lewis, *Letters to Malcolm*: *Chiefly on Prayer* (New York: Harcourt Brace & World, 1964), 75.

Chapter 10 - Can Reason Be Trusted?

1. G. K. Chesterton, *Orthodoxy* (London: Hodder and Stoughton, 1999), 55.

2. Cf. Christian Smith and Melinda Lundquist Denton, *Soul Searching: The Religious and Spiritual Lives of American Teenagers* (New York: Oxford Univ. Press, 2009).

3. Bertrand Russell, *A Free Man's Worship*, The Basic Writings of Bertrand Russell, vol. 10 (New York: Routledge, 2009), 39.

Chapter 11 - Smuggling from the Egyptians

1. Tertullian, *De Praescriptione* 7.

2. G. K. Chesterton, *Saint Thomas Aquinas* (New York: Image, 1956), 155.

3. Thomas Aquinas's idea that theology is "the queen of the sciences" is very much akin to the medieval formula "philosophy the handmaiden of theology," a conviction today largely lost, even by Christians.

4. Wendell Berry, *The Unsettling of America: Culture and Agriculture* (New York: Sierra Club, 1997), 21.

Chapter 12 - How to Know Everything

1. Cf. Edward O. Wilson, *Consilience: The Unity of Knowledge* (New York: Vintage, 1998), 13, 15.

2. Owen Barfield, *History in English Words* (London: Faber & Faber, 1953), 140.
3. Geoffrey Chaucer, "The Tale of Melibee," in *The Canterbury Tales*, trans. Peter Levi (Oxford: Oxford Univ. Press, 1985).
4. A fascinating example of this is that the very chapters by which our Bibles are still divided were first arranged by cardinal Stephen Langton in the Latin Vulgate in 1205.

Chapter 13 - A World of Desires, Not Laws

1. Clement of Alexandria, *Exhortations to the Greeks* 4.63.3.
2. Theophilus of Antioch, *To Autolycus* 2.4, 10.
3. Irenaeus, *Against Heresies* 2.30.9.
4. Martianus Capella: quoted in C. S. Lewis, *The Discarded Image* (Cambridge: Cambridge Univ. Press, 1974), 122.
5. "What we call their 'laws' seem to have been felt, not as intellectual deductions, but rather as real activities of soul—that human soul which … the philosopher could not yet feel to be wholly separate from a larger world Soul, or planetary Soul." Owen Barfield, *History in English Words* (London: Faber & Faber, 1953), 146.
6. Lucy Maud Montgomery, *Anne of Green Gables* (Reprint edition, New York: Oxford University Press, 2007), chap. 5.
7. Francis Bacon was the first to apply the modern metaphor of "laws" to natural phenomenon.
8. Cecil Day-Lewis's lines here are worth some reflection: "A scientific metaphor … like a scientific law, is valid only as long as it covers the known facts, illuminates them, and offers the most effective way of talking about them." Cecil Day-Lewis, *The Poet's Way of Knowledge* (Cambridge: Cambridge Univ. Press, 1956), 25.
9. The use of legal metaphors in the physical sciences is pervasive. Even the word *fact* comes from the Latin past participle of *facere*, "do," and was a legal term describing a deed or a crime. This is where we get the phrase "before (or after) the fact." The physical sciences did not begin to borrow this legal term to understand the world until the sixteenth century.
10. Dorothy Sayers, *The Divine Comedy*, Part 3: "Paradise" (New York: Penguin, 1962), 26.
11. Day-Lewis, *Poet's Way of Knowledge*, 5, italics mine.

12. Montgomery, *Anne of Green Gables*, chap. 5. "What's in a name? That which we call a rose / By any other name would smell as sweet." William Shakespeare, *Romeo and Juliet*, act 2, scene 2. As Owen Barfield puts it, "Prophets old" means something very different from "old prophets." Owen Barfield, *Poetic Diction: A Study in Meaning* (London: Faber & Faber, 1952), 41.

13. Dietrich Bonhoeffer, *Letters and Papers from Prison* (New York: Simon & Schuster, 1971), May 30, 1944 entry.

Chapter 15 - But Much Less Like a Ball

1. For instances of "heaven" as opposed to γη (*ge*), "earth," see Matt. 5:16, 18, 45; 23:22; Mark 1:10; 13:31; Luke 2:15; Acts 7:55–56; Col. 1:5; Heb. 12:23; Rev. 3:12. For more than one heaven, see 2 Cor. 12:2; Eph. 4:10; Heb. 1:10.

2. See, e.g., Matt. 16:2–3; Luke 17:29; Acts 2:19.

3. Cf. Gen. 15:17; Ex. 13:21; 1 Kings 18:38; 2 Kings 1:10; 1 Chron. 21:26; and also Deut. 4:24; Heb. 12:29.

4. The Sanskrit *dyaus*, the Greek *Zeus*, and the Teutonic *Tiu*.

5. Owen Barfield, *History in English Words* (London: Faber & Faber, 1953), 88–89.

6. Dallas Willard, *The Divine Conspiracy: Rediscovering Our Hidden Life in God* (New York: HarperOne, 1998), 70–71.

7. N. T. Wright, *Jesus and the Victory of God* (Minneapolis: Fortress Press, 1996), 414–21.

8. Willard, *Divine Conspiracy*, 78.

9. "O Worship the King, All Glorious Above," by Robert Grant (1833), based on the meter of W. Kethe (1561): quoted in Willard, *Divine Conspiracy*, 68.

10. N. T. Wright, *Simply Jesus* (New York: HarperOne, 2011), 199.

11. Ibid.

12. Jane Austen, *Pride and Prejudice* (Mineola, NY: Dover Publications, 1995), chap. 11.

13. William Wordsworth, *The Prelude*, Book 6: "Cambridge and the Alps," line 136 (1850).

14. Marcus Aurelius, *The Meditations* 4.23, referenced in C. S. Lewis, *The Discarded Image* (Cambridge: Cambridge Univ. Press, 1974), 203.

15. Matthew Arnold, *Thoughts on Education: Chosen from the Writings of Matthew Arnold*, ed. Leonard Huxley (New York: Macmillan, 1912), 109.
16. Barfield, *History in English Words,* 169.
17. C. S. Lewis, "The Alliterative Metre," in *Selected Literary Essays* (Cambridge: Cambridge Univ. Press, 1980), 24. *Phänomenologie des Geistes* (1807) is one of philosopher Georg Friedrich Wilhelm Hegel's most important philosophical works. Because of the dual meaning of the German *geist*, it can be translated as *The Phenomenology of Spirit* or *The Phenomenology of Mind*.
18. C. S. Lewis, *English Literature in the Sixteenth Century, Excluding Drama* (Oxford: Clarendon, 1954), 4. He said elsewhere that the universe's "true picture is to be found in the elaborate title pages of old folios where winds blow at the corners and at the bottom dolphins spout, and the eye passes upward through cities and kings and angels to four Hebrew letters with rays darting from them at the top, which represent the ineffable Name."
19. C. S. Lewis, *The Voyage of the Dawn Treader* (New York: Harper & Row, 1952), 266.
20. Some commentaries interpret the "seven stars" to mean seven lampstands or seven churches or seven angels.
21. "But when the set time had fully come, God sent his Son, born of a woman" (Gal. 4:4).

Chapter 16 - A God-Bathed World

1. John Donne, *Donne's Sermons, Selected Passages with an Essay by Logan Pearsall Smith* (Oxford: Clarendon, 1919), 160: quoted in Michael Ward, *Planet Narnia: The Seven Heavens in the Imagination of C. S. Lewis* (New York: Oxford Univ. Press, 2010), 22.
2. Dante, *The Divine Comedy*, "Paradiso," canto 33.142–45.
3. Abraham Joshua Heschel, *The Sabbath* (New York: Farrar Straus & Giroux, 2005), 101.
4. Odo, *Life of Saint Gerald of Aurillac*, 3.12. Cf. Jaroslav Pelikan, *The Growth of Medieval Theology* (Chicago: Univ. of Chicago Press, 1978), 145.
5. Boethius said, "There are three types of music. The first type is the music

of the universe (*musica mundana*), the second, that of the human being (*musica humana*), and the third type is that which is created by certain instruments (*musica intrumentis constituta*).... The music of the universe is best observed in those things which one perceives in heaven itself, or in the structure of the elements, or in the diversity of the seasons.... It is impossible that such a fast motion should produce absolutely no sound, especially since the orbits of the stars are joined by such a harmony that nothing so perfectly structured can be imagined.... Thus there must be some fixed order of musical modulation in this celestial motion": quoted in Piero Weiss and Richard Taruskin, *Music In Western Civilization: Antiquity through the Renaissance* (New York: Schirmer, 2005), 33.

6. Dorothy Sayers described it this way: "A medieval man stood upon the surface of his central earth, and gazed beyond it towards that august infinitude by Whom and in Whom and for Whom all things exist, his spiritual eye beheld, imaged by the concentric circlings of the heavenly spheres, the ninefold order, rank above rank, of the celestial Intelligences, his absolute superiors." Dorothy Sayers, *The Divine Comedy*, Part 1: "Hell" (New York: Penguin, 1959), 24.

7. From the poem "The Small Man Orders His Wedding" from C. S. Lewis, *Poems*, ed. by Walter Hooper (New York: Harcourt Brace, 1977).

8. Alexander Pope's translation of Homer, *The Iliad*, book 22, lines 38–42.

9. "He did not feel himself isolated by his skin from the world outside him to quite the same extent as we do," says Owen Barfield on the medieval man. "He was integrated or mortised into it, each different part of him being united to a different part of it by some invisible thread." Owen Barfield, *Saving the Appearances: A Study in Idolatry* (London: Faber & Faber, 1988), 78.

10. Hildegard of Bingen, *Causae et Curae*: "The firmament is like man's head: the Sun, Moon, Stars, like his eyes": quoted in Jean Seznec, *The Survival of the Pagan Gods* (Princeton: Princeton University Press, 1953), 65.

11. Lorenzo Bonincontri, *De rebus naturalibus et divinis* (About Natural and Divine Things), 2.12ff.: quoted in Seznec, *Survival of the Pagan Gods*, 82. He also writes, "Under your guidance, Jupiter shines in the sky; you restore her brilliance to Venus, and by you is Fortune obliged to diversify earthly destinies through superior influence." Bonincontri, *Dierum solemnium Christianae religionis libri* (Solemn Days of the Christian

Religion of the Book), 4.1.1.41–44: quoted in Seznec, *Survival of the Pagan Gods*, 82.

12. Michael Ward illustrates this discovery in detail in *Planet Narnia*.

13. Roger Lancelyn Green and Walter Hooper, *C. S. Lewis: A Biography* (New York: Harcourt Brace, 1974), 146.

14. There is a medieval mold with two impressions on it: one carved into the shape of a small *t*, cast to look like a Christian crucifix, and the other a capital *T*, a representation of the hammer of Thor. The idea was that Thor represented Jupiter, and Jupiter is Christlike, "Jehovah—with his thunder." William Wordsworth, "The Recluse," in *Selected Poems and Prefaces*, ed. Jack Stillinger (Boston: Houghton Mifflin, 1965).

15. C. S. Lewis, *The Planets* (New York: Harcourt Brace, 1964); cf. Ward, *Planet Narnia*, 42–76.

16. "Now Jove in next commodity of hair send thee a beard" (William Shakespeare, *Twelfth Night*, act 3, scene 5).

17. C. S. Lewis, *The Discarded Image* (Cambridge: Cambridge Univ. Press, 1974).

18. Guy Davenport, *Herakleitos and Diogenes* (Burnaby, BC: Greyfox, 1979), 21.

19. Miguel de Cervantes, *Don Quixote*, trans. John Rutherford (New York: Penguin, 2000), chap. 25.

Chapter 17 - The Love That Moves the Stars

1. G. K. Chesterton, *Orthodoxy* (London: Hodder and Stoughton, 1999), 92.

2. G. K. Chesterton, *A Defense of Nonsense* (New York: Dodd, Mead, 1911), 11.

3. Quoted in Owen Barfield, *Saving the Appearances: A Study in Idolatry* (London: Faber & Faber, 1988), 128.

4. In the nineteenth century, Scottish historian and philosopher Thomas Carlyle was the first to use *environment* in this way.

5. Edward O. Wilson, *Consilience: The Unity of Knowledge* (New York: Vintage, 1998), 232–33.

6. Two words for truth stand out in the Bible: ἀλήθεια (*aletheia*, "truth") and σοφια (*sophia*, "wisdom"); cf. Pss. 31:5; 85:10; 100:5; Mic. 7:20; Gal. 2:5, 14; Eph. 1:13; 1 Tim. 2:3–4; 2 Tim. 2:25.

7. Karl Barth, *Epistle to the Romans*: quoted in Michael Ramsey, *The Gospel and the Catholic Church* (Cambridge: Cowley, 1956), 111.

8. Dante, *The Divine Comedy*, "Paradiso," canto 33.142–45.

Chapter 18 - The Yule Log Burns

1. C. S. Lewis, *English Literature in the Sixteenth Century, Excluding Drama* (Oxford: Clarendon, 1954), 342: quoted in Michael Ward, *The Narnia Code: C. S. Lewis and the Secret of the Seven Heavens* (Carol Stream, IL: Tyndale House, 2010), 353.

Chapter 19 - A Star in Bethlehem

1. Cf. also Matt. 2:6, quoting Mic. 5:2, 4: " 'But you, Bethlehem, in the land of Judah, are by no means least among the rulers of Judah; for out of you will come a ruler who will shepherd my people Israel.' "

2. John Henry Hopkins Jr., *We Three Kings of Orient Are*, 1857.

Chapter 20 - In the Year of Our Lord

1. It takes Neptune 16.1 hours to circle the sun; Uranus, 17.2; Saturn, 10.7; Jupiter, 9.9; and Mars, 24.6. Mercury and Venus are the oddballs — Venus, especially, whose day is longer than its year (it circles the sun in 225 days but takes 243 days to spin full circle).

Chapter 21 - Deep Magic

1. Lewis says, "When I say 'magic,' I am not thinking of the paltry and pathetic techniques by which fools attempt and quacks pretend to control nature. I mean rather what is suggested in the fairy-tale sentences like 'This is a magic flower, and if you carry it, the seven gates will open to you of their own accord,' or 'This is a magic cave and those who enter it will renew their youth.' I should define magic in this sense as 'objective efficacy which cannot be further analyzed.' " C. S. Lewis, *Letters to Malcolm: Chiefly on Prayer* (New York: Harcourt Brace & World, 1964), 103. Cf. also C. S. Lewis, *The Chronicles of Narnia* (New York: Harper Collins, 2004).

Chapter 22 - Dinner at Winston's

1. 1 Cor. 12:13 (1984 NIV).

2. Owen Barfield, *History in English Words* (London: Faber & Faber, 1953), 51.

3. Charles Williams, *The Forgiveness of Sins* (Grand Rapids: Eerdmans, 1984), 136, 143.

Chapter 23 - The Spell to Break the Spell

1. Cf. John 13:1 and 18:28, which calls to mind the cry of John the Baptist in John 1:29, 36: "Look, the Lamb of God, who takes away the sin of the world!" Against this reckoning, however, in Matthew 26:17; Mark 14:12; and Luke 22:8, the Last Supper is referred to explicitly as the Passover meal.

2. Dante Alighieri, *Divine Comedy*, "Paradise," canto 33.145.

3. Origen, *Commentary on the Gospel of John*, 6.59.301.

4. Saint Cyprian, *On the Unity of the Catholic Church*, trans. Maurice Bevenot (New York: Newman Press, 1957), 6; *St. Cyprian: The Lapsed, the Unity of the Catholic Church* (New York: Newman, 1956). 49.

Chapter 24 - Re-membering

1. "The church is one," penned Optatus, "and its holiness is produced by the sacraments. It is not to be considered on the basis of the pride of individuals." Optatus, *Against Parmenianus the Donatist* 2.1: quoted in Jaroslav Pelikan, *The Emergence of the Catholic Tradition* (Chicago: Univ. of Chicago Press, 1971), 311.

2. Idelfonsus of Toledo, *On the Knowledge of Baptism* 7; Bede, *Allegorical Exposition of the Song of Songs* 3. Cf. Jaroslav Pelikan, *The Growth of Medieval Theology* (Chicago: Univ. of Chicago Press, 1978), 43. Cyril put it this way: "Let us partake as of the Body and Blood of Christ: for in the figure of Bread is given to thee his Body, and in the figure of Wine his Blood; that thou by partaking of the Body and Blood of Christ, mightest be made of the same body and the same blood with him. For thus we come to bear Christ in us, because his Body and Blood are diffused through our members; thus it is that according to the blessed Peter, *we become partakers of the divine nature*." Cyril of Jerusalem, *Catechetical Lecture* 4.3, in F. L. Cross, *Lectures on the Christian Sacraments: Saint Cyril of Jerusalem* (New York: St. Vladimir's Seminary Press, 1951), 68; cf. 2 Peter 1:4. Italics mine.

3. Dorothy Sayers, *The Divine Comedy*, Part 3: "Paradise" (New York: Penguin, 1962), 26.

4. Bonaventure, *On the Threefold Way* 2.1.2.

5. Irenaeus, *Against Heresies* 3.16.6.

6. Augustine, sermon 272, in *Patrologia latina*, ed. J.-P. Migne, 217 vols. (Paris, 1844–64): 38:1247.

7. Irenaeus, *Against Heresies* 4.18.5, in Alexander Roberts and James Donaldson, *Ante-Nicene Christian Library: Translations of the Writings of the Fathers*, vol. 1. (Edinburgh: T&T Clark, 1867), 435. He says elsewhere, "But if (those of the flesh) do not attain salvation, then neither did the Lord redeem us with his blood, nor is the cup of the Eucharist the communion of his blood, nor the bread which we break the communion of his body. . . . When, therefore, the mingled cup and the manufactured [*factus*, γεγονως, 'prepared, made'] bread receive the Word of God, and the Eucharist of the blood and the body of Christ is made, from which things the substance of our flesh is increased and supported, how can they affirm that the flesh is incapable of receiving the gift of God, which is life eternal?" Irenaeus, *Against Heresies* 5.2.2, 3, op cit. 59. Greek and Latin parenthetical from Irenaeus, *Sancti Irenaei Episcopi Lugdunensis*, trans. Aldolphus Stieren (Leipzig: n.p., 1843), 718–19.

8. των ἁγιων χοινωνια, *sanctorum communio*. By the time of the Nicene Creed, however, *sancti* are considered saints in the formal sense of having been baptized, the living *and* the dead, excluding hypocrites, but still a *communio* of persons. Cf. Werner Elert, *Eucharist and Church Fellowship in the First Four Centuries*, trans. N. E. Nagel (Saint Louis: Concordia, 1966), 7.

9. *Didache* 9.4. Michael W. Holmes, *The Apostolic Fathers: Greek Texts and English Translations*, 3rd. ed. (Grand Rapids: Baker, 2007), 359.

10. e. e. cummings, "Since feeling is first," in e. e. cummings, *Complete Poems, 1913–1962* (New York: Harcourt Brace, 1980).

11. Cyril of Jerusalem, *Catechetical Lecture* 4.6, in Cross, *Lectures on the Christian Sacraments*, 69.

Chapter 25 – Dying with Christ

1. Cf. Martin Luther: "We know that it is and is called the Lord's Supper, not the Christians' supper": quoted in Werner Elert, *Eucharist and*

Church Fellowship in the First Four Centuries, trans. N. E. Nagel (Saint Louis: Concordia, 1966), 40.

2. Augustine, *On Baptism against the Donatists* 6.10.15.

3. Cyprian, *Letters* 74.5.

4. Augustine, *Exposition of the Gospel of John* 26.18; cf. Col. 3:1–4.

5. "[Pilate] ... granted the corpse to Joseph" (Mark 15:45 ASV).

6. Owen Barfield's expression. This paragraph builds on Owen Barfield, *Saving the Appearances: A Study in Idolatry* (London: Faber & Faber, 1988), 170–73.

Chapter 26 - Death by Water

1. Sometime between 180 and 200 AD, Irenaeus, bishop of what is now Lyons, France, connected Baptism to regeneration and recapitulation, speaking of it as the "laver of regeneration." Glenn Hinson, *The Early Church: Origins to the Dawn of the Middle Ages* (Nashville: Abingdon, 1996), 79. He considered the story of the cleansing of Naaman the leper in 2 Kings 5 to be a prefiguring of Baptism, because "as we are lepers in sin, we are made clean by means of the sacred water and the invocation of the Lord, from our old transgressions, being spiritually regenerated as newborn babes." Irenaeus, *Fragments* 33: quoted in Jaroslav Pelikan, *The Emergence of the Catholic Tradition* (Chicago: University of Chicago Press, 1971), 164.

2. Darwell Stone, *Holy Baptism* (London: Longmans, Green, 1912), 42. Cf. Cyril of Jerusalem, *Procat.* 16, *Cat.* 1.3, 3.3, 4.32; Augustine, *Baptism* 1.5, 4.1, *Ep.* 185.23, *The Creed: for Catechumens* 15; Chrysostom, *In Ep. 2 ad Cor.* 3.7; Gregory of Nazianzus, *OPrat.* 40.3–4; Justin Martyr, *First Apology* 1.61, 65, *Dialogue with Trypho* 14; Basil, *Hom. in Sanc. Bapt.*, 5.

3. Cyril of Alexandria, *Glaph in Exodus* 2. Cf. J. N. D. Kelly, *Early Christian Doctrines* (New York: Harper & Row, 1960).

4. Athanasius, *Orations against the Arians* 2, 41; *On the Incarnation against Apollinaris* 14. Cf. Kelly, *Early Christian Doctrines*, 431.

5. Stanley Hauerwas wrote: "The sacraments enact the story of Jesus and, thus, form a community in his image. We could not be the church without them. For the story of Jesus is not simply one that is told: it must be enacted. The sacraments are means crucial to shaping and preparing us

to tell and hear that story. Thus baptism is that rite of initiation necessary for us to become part of Jesus' death and resurrection. Through baptism we do not simply learn the story, but we become part of that story." Stanley Hauerwas, *The Peaceable Kingdom* (Notre Dame: University of Notre Dame Press, 1983), 107–8.

Chapter 28 - Reorienting Our Loves

1. I owe this idea to N. T. Wright, in his preface to *The New Testament and the People of God* (Minneapolis: Fortress, 1992).

2. Lesslie Newbigin, *The Gospel in a Pluralist Society* (Grand Rapids: Eerdmans, 1989), 9.

3. In Mark, σχιζω (*schizo*), "to tear, to rend," appears only at Jesus' baptism when the skies are "torn open" (Mark 1:10) and at Jesus' death when the temple curtain is "torn in two" (Mark 15:38).

4. Augustine, *City of God* 11.1; cf. Jaroslav Pelikan, *The Growth of Medieval Theology* (Chicago: Univ. of Chicago Press, 1978), 2.

5. Julian of Toledo, *Antitheses* 2.69; cf. Pelikan, *Growth of Medieval Theology*, 2.

6. With much gratitude, I owe this interpretation of Luke 14:26 to a sermon by Father Steve Schlossberg.

Chapter 30 - A Holy Renaissance

1. "The kingdom of God is the redemptive reign of God dynamically active to establish his rule among human beings.... This kingdom, which will appear as an apocalyptic act at the end of the age, has already come into human history in the person and mission of Jesus to overcome evil, to deliver people from its power, and to bring them into the blessings of God's reign. The kingdom of God involves two great moments: fulfillment within history and consummation at the end of history." George Eldon Ladd, *A Theology of the New Testament,* rev. ed. (Grand Rapids: Eerdmans, 1993), 89–90.

Bibliography

Ambrose. *On the Mysteries*. Translated by B. D. Thompson. New York: Macmillan, 1919.

Austen, Jane. *Pride and Prejudice*. Mineola, NY: Dover Publications, 1995.

Barfield, Owen. *History in English Words*. Grand Rapids: Eerdmans, 1967.

―――. *Poetic Diction: A Study of Meaning*. Middletown, CT: Wesleyan Universtiy Press, 1973.

―――. *Saving the Appearances: A Study in Idolatry*. London: Faber & Faber, 1988.

Barnard, William Leslie. *St. Justin Martyr: The First and Second Apologies*. New York: Paulist, 1997.

Basil. *Ascetical Works*. Translated by M. M. Wagner. Washington, DC: Catholic Univ. of America Press, 1970.

Berger, Peter L. *The Sacred Canopy: Elements of a Sociological Theory of Religion*. New York: Doubleday, 1967.

Berger, Peter L., and Thomas Luckmann. *The Social Construction of Reality: A Treatise in the Sociology of Knowledge*. New York: Doubleday, 1966.

Bobrick, Benson. *The Fated Sky: Astrology in History*. New York: Simon & Schuster, 2005.

Bradshaw, Paul. *Eucharistic Origins*. Oxford: Oxford Univ. Press, 2004.

Brent, Allen. *St. Cyprian of Carthage: On the Church: Select Letters*. Crestwood, NY: St. Vladimir's Seminary Press, 2006.

Bultmann, Rudolph. *Jesus Christ and Mythology*. New York: Scribner, 1958.

Cervantes, Miguel de. *Don Quixote*. Translated by John Rutherford. New York: Penguin, 2000.

Chargaff, Erwin. *Heraclitean Fire*. New York: Rockefeller Univ. Press, 1978.

―――. *Voices in the Labyrinth: Nature, Man, and Science*. New York: Seabury, 1977.

Chaucer, Geoffrey. *The Canterbury Tales*. Translated by Peter Levi. Oxford: Oxford Univ. Press, 1985.

Chesterton, G. K. *A Defense of Nonsense*. New York: Dodd, Mead, 1911.

———. *Orthodoxy*. London: Hodder and Stoughton, 1999.

———. *St. Thomas Aquinas*. New York: Image, 1956.

Chittister, Joan. *The Liturgical Year*. Nashville: Thomas Nelson, 2009.

Chrysostom, John. *The Divine Liturgy*. London: Faith, 1951.

Clarke, W. K. Lowther, ed. *Liturgy and Worship: A Companion to the Prayer Books of the Anglican Communion*. London: SPCK, 1959.

Crawford, Matthew R. *The Lord's Supper: Remembering and Proclaiming Christ until He Comes*. Nashville: B & H, 2010.

Cross, F. L. *Lectures on the Christian Sacraments: Saint Cyril of Jerusalem*. New York: St. Vladimir's Seminary Press, 1951.

"A Darling Little Duck," by "the author of 'Cobwebs,' etc. etc." in *Peterson's Magazine* 69 and 70 (1876).

Davenport, Guy. *Herakleitos and Diogenes*. Burnaby, BC: Greyfox, 1979.

Dawkins, Richard. *A Devil's Chaplain: Reflections on Hope, Lies, Science, and Love*. New York: Houghton Mifflin, 2003.

———. *River Out of Eden: A Darwinian View of Life*. New York: Basic, 1995.

Day-Lewis, Cecil. *The Poet's Way of Knowledge*. Cambridge: Cambridge Univ. Press, 1956.

Delorme, J. *The Eucharist in the New Testament*. Baltimore: Helicon, 1964.

Descartes, Rene. *Discourse on Method and Meditations on First Philosophy*. Indianapolis: Hackett, 1998.

Dix, Gregory. *The Shape of the Liturgy*, Glasgow: Dacre, 1945.

Donne, John. *The Major Works*. Edited by John Carey. New York: Oxford Univ. Press, 1990.

Easton, Burton Scott. *The Apostolic Tradition of Hippolytus*. Cambridge: Cambridge Univ. Press, 1934.

Elert, Werner. *Eucharist and Church Fellowship in the First Four Centuries*. Translated by N. E. Nagel. Saint Louis: Concordia, 1966.

Eliot, T. S. *Complete Poems and Plays 1909–1950*. New York: Harcourt Brace, 1967.

Fortescue, Adrian. *The Mass: A Study of the Roman Liturgy*. New York: Longmans, Green, 1930.

Funkenstein, Amos. *Theology and the Scientific Imagination from the Middle Ages to the Seventeenth Century.* Princeton: Princeton Univ. Press, 1986.

Gross, Bobby. *Living the Christian Year.* Downers Grove, IL: InterVarsity, 2009.

Harris, Sam. *The End of Faith: Religion, Terror, and the Future of Reason.* W. W. Norton, 2004.

Hauerwas, Stanley. *The Peaceable Kingdom.* Notre Dame, IN: Univ. of Notre Dame Press, 1983.

Hauerwas, Stanley, and William Willimon. *Resident Aliens.* Nashville: Abingdon, 1989.

Heschel, Abraham Joshua. *The Sabbath.* New York: Farrar, Straus, 2005.

Hinson, Glenn. *The Early Church: Origins to the Dawn of the Middle Ages.* Nashville: Abingdon, 1996.

Holmes, Michael W. *The Apostolic Fathers: Greek Texts and English Translations*, 3rd ed. Grand Rapids: Baker, 2007.

Hopkins, Gerard Manley. *Poems and Prose.* New York: Penguin, 1963.

Ireton, Kimberlee Conway. *The Circle of Seasons.* Downers Grove, IL: InterVarsity, 2008.

Judge, Michael. *The Dance of Time.* New York: MJF, 2004.

Kelly, J. M. D., *Early Christian Doctrines.* New York: Harper & Row, 1960.

Kereszty, Roch. *Wedding Feast of the Lamb.* Chicago: Hillenbrand: 2004.

Kilmartin, Edward J. *The Eucharist in the West.* Collegeville, MN: Liturgical, 1998.

Kuhn, Thomas. *The Structure of Scientific Revolutions.* Chicago: Univ. of Chicago Press, 1996.

Levine, Robert. *A Geography of Time.* New York: Basic, 1997.

Levy, David H., and John O'Bryne. *Practical Skywatching.* San Francisco: Fog City, 2002.

Lewis, C. S. *The Discarded Image.* Cambridge: Cambridge Univ. Press, 1974.

————. *English Literature in the Sixteenth Century, Excluding Drama.* Oxford: Clarendon, 1954.

————. *God in the Dock.* Edited by Walter Hooper. Grand Rapids: Eerdmans, 1970.

————. *Letters to Malcolm: Chiefly on Prayer.* New York: Harcourt, Brace, and World, 1964.

————. *The Lion, the Witch, and the Wardrobe.* New York: Harper & Row, 1950, 68.

————. *Miracles.* New York: HarperOne, 1996.

————. *Poems.* New York: Harcourt Brace, 1964.

————. *A Preface to Paradise Lost.* New York: Oxford Univ. Press, 1961.

————. *Selected Literary Essays.* Cambridge: Cambridge Univ. Press, 1980.

————. *Studies in Words.* Cambridge: Cambridge Univ. Press, 1967.

————. *Surprised by Joy.* London: Geoffrey Bles, 1955.

————. *Transposition and Other Addresses.* London: Geoffrey Bles, 1949.

Lydgate, John, and Frederick James Furnivall. *Lydgate's Reson and Sensuallyte.* Vol. 1, p. 98. Lines 1438, 3091; 3103.

MacDonald, George. *Diary of an Old Soul.* Minneapolis: Augsburg, 1989.

Macgregor, G. H. C. *Eucharistic Origins.* London: James Clarke, 1928.

MacMullen, Ramsay. *Paganism in the Roman Empire.* New Haven: Yale Univ. Press, 1981.

Macy, Gary. *The Banquet's Wisdom: A Short History of the Theologies of the Lord's Supper.* New York: Paulist, 1992.

————. *Treasures from the Storeroom: Medieval Religion and the Eucharist.* Collegeville, MN: Liturgical, 1999.

Maritain, Jacques, and Raissa Maritain, *The Complete Works (1906–1920) in 15 Volumes.* Vol. 9. Paris: Saint-Paul, 1990.

McEntyre, Marilyn Chandler. *Caring for Words in a Culture of Lies.* Grand Rapids: Eerdmans, 2009.

McKinion, Steven. *Life and Practice in the Early Church: A Documentary Reader.* New York: New York Univ. Press, 2001.

Michel, G. A. *Landmarks in Liturgy.* London: Darton Longman and Todd, 1961.

Milton, John. *Paradise Lost.* Edited by Alastair Fowler. London: Longman, 1998.

Molnar, Michael R. *The Star of Bethlehem: The Legacy of the Magi.* New Brunswick, NJ: Rutgers Univ. Press, 2000.

Montgomery, Lucy Maud. *Anne of Green Gables*. Reprint edition. New York: Oxford University Press, 2007, chap. 5.

Nagel, N. E. *Eucharist and Church Fellowship in the First Four Centuries*. Saint Louis: Concordia, 1966.

Newbigin, Lesslie. *The Gospel in a Pluralist Society*. Grand Rapids: Eerdmans, 1989.

Noth, Martin. *Numbers: A Commentary*. Philadelphia: Westminster, 1968.

Perse, Saint-John. *On Poetry*. Translated by W. H. Auden. New York: Bollingen Foundation, 1961.

Pick, Bernhard. *The Apocryphal Acts of Paul, Peter, John, Andrew and Thomas*. Chicago: Open Court, 1909.

Pieper, Josef. *Faith, Hope, Love*. San Francisco: Ignatius, 1997.

Pope, Alexander. *An Essay on Criticism*. Cambridge: Cambridge University Press, 1908.

Radbertus, Paschasius. *The Book of Bertram: Body and Blood of the Lord*. Translated by W. F. Taylor. London: Simpkin Marshall, 1880.

Ramsey, Arthur Michael. *The Gospel and the Catholic Church*. New York: Longmans, Green, 1937.

Randles, W. G. L. *The Unmaking of the Medieval Christian Cosmos, 1500–1760: From Solid Heavens to Boundless Aether*. Brookfield, VT: Ashgate, 1999.

Ratramnus, *The Body and Blood of the Lord*. Translated by George Englert McCracken. In *Early Medieval Theology*. Library of Christian Classics. Vol. 9. Philadelphia: Westminster, 1957.

Riggans, Walter. *Numbers*. Philadelphia: Westminster, 1983.

Roberts, Alexander, and James Donaldson. *Ante-Nicene Christian Library: Translations of the Writings of the Fathers*. Vol. 2. Edinburgh: T&T Clark, 1867.

Schaff, Philip, and David Schley Schaff. *History of the Christian Church, Volume I: Apostolic Christianity. A.D. 1–100*. New York: Scribner, 1882.

Scotland, N. A. D. *Eucharistic Consecration in the First Four Centuries and Its Implications for Liturgical Reform*. Oxford: Latimer House, 1989.

Sertillanges, A. G. *The Intellectual Life: Its Spirit, Conditions, Methods*. Translated by Mary Ryan. Westminster, MD: Newman Press, 1946.

Seznec, Jean. *The Survival of the Pagan Gods*. Princeton: Princeton Univ. Press, 1953.

Smith, Christian, and Denton, Melinda Lundquist. *Soul Searching: The Religious and Spiritual Lives of American Teenagers*. New York: Oxford Univ. Press, 2009.

Stieren, Adolphus. *Irenaeus: Sancti Irenaei Episcopi Lugdunensis*. Leipzig, Germany: n.p., 1843.

Taylor, James S. *Poetic Knowledge*. New York: State Univ. of New York Press, 1998.

Teilhard de Chardin, Pierre. *The Phenomenon of Man* (New York: Fontana, 1959).

Thompson, C. J. S. *The Mystery and Romance of Astrology*. New York: Causeway, 1973.

Tippett, Krista. *Einstein's God*. New York: Penguin, 2010.

Turgenev, Ivan. *Fathers and Sons*. New York: Airmont, 1967.

Ward, Michael. *The Narnia Code: C. S. Lewis and the Secret of the Seven Heavens*. Carol Stream, IL: Tyndale House, 2010.

———. *Planet Narnia: The Seven Heavens in the Imagination of C. S. Lewis*. Oxford: Oxford Univ. Press, 2008.

Weiss, Piero, and Richard Taruskin. *Music in Western Civilization: Antiquity through the Renaissance*. New York: Schirmer, 2005.

Wells, Amy Catherine. *The Book of Catherine Wells*, 22, introduction by H. G. Wells. Garden City, NY: Doubleday, Doran, 1928.

Wenham, Gordon J. *Numbers: An Introduction and Commentary*. Downers Grove, IL: InterVarsity, 1981.

Willard, Dallas. *The Divine Conspiracy: Rediscovering Our Hidden Life in God*. New York: HarperOne, 1998.

———. *Knowing Christ Today*. New York: HarperOne, 2009.

Williams, Charles. *The Figure of Beatrice*. Berkeley, CA: Apocryphile, 2005.

———. *He Came Down from Heaven and The Forgiveness of Sins*. Berkeley, CA: Apocryphile, 2005.

Wilson, Edward O. *Consilience: The Unity of Knowledge*. New York: Vintage, 1998.

———. *On Human Nature*. Cambridge: Harvard Univ. Press, 1978.

Witham, Larry. *The Measure of God*. New York: HarperCollins, 2005.

Wordsworth, William. *Selected Poems and Prefaces*. Edited by Jack Stillinger. Boston: Houghton Mifflin, 1965.

Wright, N. T. *Jesus and the Victory of God*. Minneapolis: Fortress, 1996.

————. *The New Testament and the People of God*. Minneapolis: Fortress, 1992.

————. *Simply Jesus*. New York: HarperOne, 2011.

Zerubavel, Eviatar. *The Seven Day Circle: The History and Meaning of the Week*. Chicago: Univ. of Chicago Press, 1985.